Becoming Friends

WB/WG

Becoming Friends

Worship, Justice, and the Practice
of Christian Friendship

Paul J. Wadell

Brazos Press
A Division of Baker Book House Co
Grand Rapids, Michigan 49516

Published by Brazos Press
a division of Baker Book House Company
P.O. Box 6287, Grand Rapids, MI 49516–6287

Printed in the United States of America

Library of Congress Cataloging-in-Publication Data

Wadell, Paul J.
    Becoming friends : worship, justice, and the practice of Christian friendship / Paul J. Wadell.
        p.   cm.
    Includes bibliographical references.
    ISBN 1-58743-051-7 (pbk.)
    1. God—Worship and love. 2. Friendship—Religious aspects— Christianity. 3. Christian life—Catholic authors. I. Title.
    BV4817 .W32 2002
    241′.6762—dc21   2002002818

For current information about all releases from Brazos Press, visit our web site:
http://www.brazospress.com

To Carmella

Contents

Introduction

Every book is born somewhere, and I would trace the origin of this one to a library carrel at the University of Notre Dame. Many years ago I was a graduate student there, and it was while preparing for my doctoral exams that I became friends with the great Catholic theologian of the thirteenth century, Thomas Aquinas. It may seem strange to claim as one of your best friends a man who has been dead for over seven hundred years, but believe me, I spent more time with Aquinas in the pages of his *Summa Theologiae* those days than I did with anyone living, and by the time I took the exams felt I knew him well enough to consider him a friend. Of course, it is convenient to claim someone long dead as a friend because he can hardly protest my presumption, but I felt a deep kinship with Aquinas because his understanding of the Christian life made remarkable sense to me.

This was especially true when I read what he said about friendship, particularly friendship with God. The cornerstone of Aquinas's theological edifice—specifically his account of the Christian life—is the virtue of charity. That in itself is not surprising since the apostle Paul makes a similar claim in his eloquent panegyric to love in 1 Corinthians 13, but what fascinated me about Aquinas's treatment of the love called charity is that he described charity as a life of friendship with God. It is such a beautiful, uplifting, and hopeful way to understand the Christian life, and one I found immediately appealing. I wondered

what this image might mean for how we think about the church.
Could the church best be understood as the community of the
friends of God? Is this a fitting image of what the church is called
to be?

Still, despite the attractive power of this metaphor, I was
uneasy because it risks an elitism that should never characterize the church. For instance, if Christians are the friends of God,
what does this say about everybody else? Furthermore, to speak
of the church as the community of the friends of God risks the
awful temptation of thinking the church must already be perfect and complete, and anyone with an eye half open knows that
is hardly true. Nonetheless, despite these misgivings, I was convinced this was not only a very promising way to think about
the church but also a fittingly challenging way. To speak of
friendship with God can sound so cozy and consoling, as if we
are all snuggling up to God; however, there is no riskier vulnerability than to live in friendship with God, because every friendship changes us, because friends have expectations of each other,
and because friends are said to be committed to the same things.
Suddenly the metaphor was not so comforting because it suggests that any friend of God is called to faithfully embody the
ways of God in the world, even to the point of suffering on
account of them. There may be grace and glory in being a friend
of God, but there is also clearly a cost.

Aquinas suggests this when he speaks of the "effects of charity," namely the consequences of living in friendship with God.
He envisioned charity not only as a singular virtue an individual might possess but also as a communal way of life. For him,
friendship with God is not a solitary enterprise but something
the baptized are to pursue together. We join the community of
the friends of God through baptism, and we nurture and sustain this life through the prayer and practices of the church. Living a life of friendship with God in the community of the baptized is inescapably transformative. It not only gives us a new
identity but also makes the church a community of unmistakable character. Aquinas described this character as the "effects
of charity" and named these effects joy, peace, mercy, kindness,
almsgiving, and fraternal correction. The list is not exhaustive
but does emphasize that a life of friendship with God should
create a church of distinctive character and witness and, there-

fore, special responsibilities. At the very least it suggests that people should be able to look to the church and see embodied there genuine joy, peace, mercy, kindness, generosity, hospitality, and a people who are not afraid to be truthful with one another. What a gift the church could be if people really could see these qualities alive in it today.

Aquinas does one more thing that explains the shape of this book. He speaks of the Eucharist as the "sacrament of charity," the setting in which a life of friendship with God is best learned, nurtured, and celebrated. Again, a nifty image with decisive implications. Aquinas hints that we do not first understand the Christian life and then worship, but that it is only in the liturgy and worship of the church that we can grasp what living in friendship with God means and what it demands of our lives. Theologians often bemoan the separation between liturgy and Christian morality, unsure what the connection might be, but Aquinas points a way by claiming that Christian morality is not only inseparable from worship, it begins there. It is through the prayer and worship of the church that we are initiated into a life of friendship with God and gradually embody the characteristics of a friend of God.

The purpose of this book is not to revisit Aquinas but to probe the implications of his thought for how we understand our Christian lives today and for how we envision what the church ought to be. Following Aquinas, I shall suggest that worship and ethics are indissolubly linked, because it is through the rituals and practices of Christian worship that we discern the shape of the Christian life and begin to acquire the virtues and dispositions that are essential to that life. Put differently, what we think the church should be and how we think Christians ought to live hinge on what we think should happen when we worship. Maybe one of the reasons there are so many conflicting ideas among Christians about what our communal life should be is because we have so many different opinions about what our worship should be. I am Roman Catholic and sometimes wonder what would happen if one Sunday we stopped in the middle of the Eucharist and asked everyone what they thought we were doing and why we were doing it. I suspect the responses to these questions might be quite different, even incompatible. We have conflicting ideas about what our worship should be, and so we have conflicting ideas about what our shared life as Christians should be.

This book may not resolve that dilemma, but hopefully it will offer a promising alternative. Like Aquinas, I propose that the liturgy and worship of the church should form us into a community whose lives truly do give glory and praise to God because our prayer has formed us into the friends of God. Becoming such a community should impact every dimension of our lives, including how we understand all the relationships of our lives. Friendship with God should illumine and guide our friendships with others, giving us important insights about intimacy, about the qualities of good relationships, about being able to distinguish between authentic friendships and counterfeit friendships, about befriending the misfits and strangers who come our way, and perhaps most important, about the purposes of the best relationships of our lives. Thus, the opening chapter of the book will explore the role of liturgy and worship in tutoring us in the practices of friendship with God. Chapters 2 and 3 will look at some common obstacles and barriers to intimacy and friendship, the qualities of authentic friendship, and some of the many good things that good friends do for us. The fourth and fifth chapters will offer a theological analysis of friendship by considering how Christians should think about friendship and how they should understand its place in the Christian life, especially in a life of discipleship with Christ.

All of this is certainly important, but friendship with God cannot be confined to those near and dear to us. If the church is to be a community of the friends of God, it must reach out to others through the witness and practice of certain virtues. There are many ways the church is called to continue the mission and ministry of Jesus, but one of the most urgent today is to be a community that embodies in its life together the virtues, dispositions, and practices displayed by Jesus in the gospel. If Christians faithfully embrace the rigors of discipleship and become "sacraments" of Christ in the world, the church will truly be a community of salvation that presents a way of life that is rich in grace and full of hope. The final chapters of the book will examine some of the virtues Christians are summoned to exemplify in their lives together today.

Writing a book reminds me of how indebted we are to others. Earlier versions of chapters 1, 4, and 6 were given as part of the Kershner Lectures at Emmanuel School of Religion in Johnson City, Tennessee. I am most grateful to Dr. Fred Norris, who first approached me about the Kershner Lectures, and to the faculty and students of Emmanuel for the insights, questions, and suggestions they raised in response to the lectures. Even more important, I am indebted to Emmanuel School of Religion for showing me what a true worshiping community should be and what it means to be a church. The hospitality, warmth, friendship, and support I found with them continue to shape me.

Phil Kenneson, a professor of theology at Milligan College, attended those lectures and suggested I might develop them into a book. Anyone who has read his *Life on the Vine* will see his influence on the tone, shape, and direction of this book. I am indebted to him for the encouragement and suggestions he offered when I was trying to figure out what this book should be. Likewise, abundant thanks are owed Rodney Clapp and Rebecca Cooper, as well as the entire staff of Brazos Press. The suggestions and guidance they offered gave me a better idea of how to write this book, and Rodney Clapp's patient and careful editing made it much more readable than it otherwise would have been.

For the past few years I have been on the faculty of St. Norbert College in De Pere, Wisconsin, a splendid place to teach, to write, and to learn about friendship. Studying theology is wonderful, but even better when you can enjoy doing it with friends, and that is what I have found with my colleagues in religious studies at St. Norbert College. And there are the students. There is no better way to find out if your ideas are worth repeating than to share them with students. So much of what unfolds in these pages first came to life in the always unpredictable cauldron of the classroom. I am grateful to all of my students, especially those in "Doing Theology Today" and "Sexuality, Intimacy, and God." Their questions, responses, and occasional challenges helped clarify what I thought I should say and how I should go about saying it. Much that is presented here about what the church should be, about the meaning and importance of friendship, and about why we need to have certain virtues in order to flourish together as friends of God was written with these students in mind.

Finally, there is Carmella. I have always believed that in order to discern the activity of God in our lives we have to learn to "read the signs," even if that means paying attention to a fortune cookie. Not long ago I cracked open a fortune cookie and was told, "Stop searching forever. Happiness is just next to you." Carmella has proven that, and so many other things, true. I may miss some of the graces that come my way, but I am glad I embraced this one. Studs Terkel once said, "Take it as it comes, but take it." I am glad I "took" Carmella and, more important, that she "took" me. This book is part of a lifelong thanks to her.

one

Worshiping Dangerously

The Risky Business of Becoming Friends of God

Many years ago when I was first teaching in Chicago, Stanley Hauerwas, then a professor at the University of Notre Dame, came to our school for a lecture. In a discussion that evening with some of the faculty, Hauerwas was asked what he thought about the U.S. Catholic bishops' then recently released pastoral, *The Challenge of Peace*. Hauerwas responded that he was impressed with the document but regretted the bishops had not asked more of American Catholics. He wished the bishops had gone further by challenging American Catholics to see pacifism not as a gospel option but as integral to a life of faithful discipleship. When the questioner suggested American Catholics would never accept pacifism as a requirement of faith, Hauerwas, a Methodist, responded, "You Catholics go to Mass all the time. What do all those Masses do for you?"

It was vintage Hauerwas—a response only he would think to give—and his question stayed with me for a long time. What does worship do for us? If we find ourselves in communities of worship week after week, has it made a difference in our lives? Has it changed us? Has it made us see the world differently? Has all our worship had any lasting transformative effect, or does

15

worship comfort us in ways that are misleading? Have we made worship safe and, therefore, empty?

These questions go to the heart of the relationship between Christian worship and the Christian moral life. Worship and morality share a common goal: both want to initiate us into the truth of Jesus so we can become as much like God as we possibly can, so resplendent in holiness and goodness that we walk the earth no longer as strangers or foes of God but as the loyal, faithful friends of God, a people committed to living for the plans and purposes of God. The strategies of Christian worship and Christian morality are one. Both seek to bring God fully to life in us and in our world. Both work to remove all the things that obstruct the full unfolding of God in our midst, whether that be in our hearts, in our relationships, in our communities, or in the structures, practices, and institutions of society.

But true Christian worship is dangerous, far more a risk than a consolation, because true Christian worship initiates us into the stories and practices of a God whose ways are so maddeningly different from our own and, therefore, full of hope. True Christian worship allows God to go to work on us, sanctifying us, gracing us, purifying, renewing, and reforming us; indeed, doing all that is necessary to make us new creatures in Christ. Nobody should enter into worship and remain unchanged, because the graced power of worship is to make us vulnerable to the God who has ceaselessly been vulnerable to us in covenant, in grace, in Christ and the Spirit, and in sacrament. Put differently, if we worship faithfully, those who knew us in our "former lives" should hardly recognize us in our new lives. This is why from the beginning the church has described this startling transformation as a death and rebirth, as a burial of one way of living, thinking, perceiving, and acting and a resurrection into a radically new kind of life that is gracious and abounding in hope because it is life in, with, and according to Christ.

The ongoing effect of Christian liturgy and worship should be to form us, the church, into communities of friends of God. This is not quaint, pious sentiment but the most accurate and captivating way to describe the radical change of self and community faithful worship should engender. We are not naturally friends of God because we do not naturally seek the ways of God, or we approach our relationship with God in the same way we

approach so many other relationships of our lives—as something we can control, limit, direct, and manipulate according to
our own interests and plans. Consequently, we become as deft
at exploiting God as we are at exploiting others.

Authentic friendship is notoriously different and inescapably
risky. True friendships are not relationships we control but
adventures we enter into; indeed, friendship is more a surrender than a conquest, more a loss of control than a calculated
plan. Friendship is a matter of mutual affection, of reciprocal
love, care, and concern. It is also a matter of shared vision, of
similar beliefs and convictions. Every friendship is an adventure, a journey perhaps, that changes us over time, shaping our
character, forming our habits, cultivating in us attitudes and
dispositions that stand as an inventory of the relationships we
have had and the effect they have had on us.

Christian liturgy and worship should form the church into a
community of friends of God. Such a hopeful and magnanimous
way of understanding our lives is also ineluctably risky because
to live in friendship with God is to will what God wills, to seek
what God seeks, and through a lifetime of faithful, committed
love, to become one with a God who has a dream for the world
we often strangely fear, a dream Christians call the reign of God.
Ultimately, the goal of Christian worship is to create and sustain a community of friends of God who *precisely because they
are friends of God* commit themselves to embodying and proclaiming and practicing the ways of God's reign in the world.
Such a life is not without risk—the faith of the martyrs attests
this—but it is the *vocation of the friends of God*, a vocation into
which we are initiated as we learn and practice the ways of Jesus,
the perfect embodiment and exemplar of friendship with God.

In this opening chapter we will explore how the worship and
liturgy of the church should form us in friendship with God and
make us into a community committed to carrying on the mission and ministry of God. But as Hauerwas's question intimates,
sometimes "all those Masses" do little for us because we approach worship as something safe and comfortable and constantly reassuring, and not as the setting in which we learn "the
dangerous ways of God" that come to us in Christ. Thus, we shall
first examine how Christians can manipulate, deform, and sab-
otage worship so that it becomes less an act of genuine praise

and more a ritual of hopeless consolation. Second, we shall reflect on why the heart of Christian worship is the risky endeavor of learning the language of God that comes to us in Christ, a language that forms us in friendship with God. Third, we shall consider two ways a life of friendship with God summons the Christian community to serve the world.

From Sham Worship to True Worship

In their book *People of the Truth*, Robert Webber and Rodney Clapp say worship should form Christians into a people of distinctive identity and vision, an identity and vision that I suggest is best expressed by friendship with God. This redemptive transformation can occur only when we open ourselves to the full power and promise of the liturgy. Too often, Webber and Clapp suggest, churches try to tame the liberating power of worship by making it something we defuse and control instead of something that provokes, challenges, and changes us. We make worship safe and predictably soothing, a practice designed to assure us that all is already well with us in lives that are already pleasing to God. We enter worship confident that our hearts can remain untouched and our spirits unexposed, and we leave, not surprisingly, unshaken and unchanged. In such a scenario, worship becomes a weekly massage for the ego, not the ritual that initiates us into the often unnerving disciplines of discipleship and the redemptive practices of God.[1]

Or we turn worship into entertainment, thinking good worship is not necessarily one that praises God but one at which the congregation applauds at least once, laughs agreeably at well-timed jokes in the sermon, and leaves us upbeat and smiling. This trivializes worship because it shifts our attention from the narratives of God and the compelling challenges those narratives present to us to strategies that make worship a hopefully pleasing pastime (much like going to the movies) but not a ritual that can empower us to live in hope. No wonder a growing number of people, particularly the young, experience worship as tediously boring and eminently forgettable. Once we believe worship has to be entertaining and amusing in order to be worthwhile, are we not secretly acknowledging we no longer believe that the stories of God we find in the Scriptures are captivating enough to merit our attention? Or that the God who comes to us in the Eucharist is sufficient nourishment for our hearts? Or, more seriously, that what happens at the Eucharist is finally neither important nor believable and thus must be enhanced by something else?

When liturgy becomes entertainment, our worship becomes as trivial as our lives. The aim of such liturgies is not to unleash the power of God in our lives and in our world but to keep God as safely remote as possible precisely because we fear what any real encounter with God might bring. In short, when the dynamics of our entertainment culture determine the shape of our worship, we manipulate God so that God becomes pleasing to us instead of us becoming pleasing to God.

There is a scene in Walker Percy's novel *Love in the Ruins* that captures this. One of the characters in the novel is Fr. Rinaldo Smith, pastor at St. Michael's Church. One Sunday morning Fr. Smith steps into the pulpit to begin his sermon, but instead of speaking he falls silent. The priest stands there not saying a word. For thirty seconds he looks out on his increasingly baffled congregation but doesn't open his mouth and, as Percy observes, "Nothing is more uncomfortable than silence when speech is expected."[2] The people begin "to cough and shift around in the pews,"[3] wondering what is wrong with their pastor.

Finally, Fr. Smith breaks the silence by saying, "Excuse me, but the channels are jammed and the word is not getting through."[4] The relieved parishioners think he is talking about troubles with the sound system and are reassured, but their comfort fades because instead of continuing with the service, Fr. Smith steps down from the pulpit, walks out of the sanctuary and, fully vested, returns to the rectory.

Percy's fictional priest knows that sometimes the "channels" of our lives are so jammed by our needs, desires, preferences, anxieties, and concerns that the Word of God cannot break through. In *People of the Truth*, Webber and Clapp call this "sham worship," the kind of worship that masquerades at praising God but whose real intent is to celebrate and compliment ourselves.[5] In sham worship we are the center of attention, not God, and God is admitted into worship only insofar as God is useful to us. As Fr. Smith's hasty retreat from the church indicated, sham worship is not only dishonest but is also a colossal waste of time.

There is a crucial difference between entertainment and celebration, between sham worship and genuine praise. Praise is born from wonder and gratitude for the goodness of God. Praise is evoked by thanksgiving for the unending generosity of God and amazement for the saving deeds of God. In genuine praise and celebration our attention is drawn to God, not ourselves; in fact, it is exactly this attentiveness to God that frees us from such enervating preoccupation with ourselves. Moreover, there is a dangerous deception behind entertainment once it becomes culturally baptized as a fitting way of life, namely the suggestion that to be human is to be continually distracted and amused. In a culture in which entertainment is approached with religious zeal, everyone, including God, has an obligation to please us.

Liturgy and worship should be about praising God and celebrating the goodness and faithfulness of God. Worship ought to be liberating precisely because to praise God is to be drawn out of ourselves and into the stories and narratives of God. With worship we *enter into the world of God* so we can come to know the ways of God and become active participants in the reign of God. Entertainment asks nothing of us, but worship asks for our lives. Entertainment tells us we have a right to be gratified, but real worship reminds us that our lives are not our own, they are God's, and God summons us to be part of the ongoing story of God that has come to us through Israel and Jesus.

Entertainment distracts us from the pressing obligations of life, but real worship cultivates in us not only a sense of indebtedness but also of "requiredness."[6] Real worship reminds us that to be human is to be summoned, to be entrusted with a task. Real worship suggests the fundamental question of life is not "What are my rights?" or "How can everyone and everything please me?" but "What is demanded of me?" and "How does God depend on me?" As Abraham Heschel so presciently observed, "To celebrate is to share in a greater joy, to participate in an eternal drama. In acts of consumption the intention is to please our own selves; in acts of celebration the intention is to extol God, the spirit, the source of blessing."[7]

As Heschel's comments indicate, entertainment is a species of consumerism, and much of contemporary worship has been taken over by the logic and categories of consumerism. In the logic of consumerism, the pastor or minister becomes not the leader of a community of faith who is summoned to call that community to greater faithfulness in discipleship but a salesperson trying to market a product to a congregation. The congregation in turn sees itself not primarily as the people of God but as a group of diverse and very demanding consumers whose needs often conflict. When worship becomes captive to consumerism, you need a God people will like and a message they are willing to buy. Instead of telling a congregation they must grow in conformity to Christ and see their lives as an ongoing conversion of heart, in consumerist Christianity it is the gospel that must conform to the needs, interests, and fancies of the congregation. It is the message of Christ, not the Christian, that must be adjusted whenever what Christ asks of us is unpalatable. The result is a Christianity with no power and no promise, a Christianity not sufficiently "dangerous" to be hopeful. Wherever such congregations exist we find not a community of the friends of God but an assortment of isolated and often divisive individuals whose lives are connected by nothing more than the slender thread of choice.

If we experience worship as safe, as something that never rocks our world or shakes us out of our normal habits of feeling, seeing, thinking, and behaving, we may be consoled but we shall never be redeemed. As a line from Eucharistic Prayer C in the Episcopal *Book of Common Prayer* implores, "Deliver us from the presumption of coming to this Table for solace only, and not for strength; for pardon only, and not for renewal." Accordingly, Webber and Clapp note, true worship, like God, may be good but it is never safe.[8] True worship is risky because through it we become increasingly vulnerable to the love and goodness of God, a love and goodness that can be so powerfully transformative that through it we gradually acquire a new identity and a new way of life.

Through worship, then, we are to see ourselves not as consumers and not as self-interested individuals, but as *a people, a community* formed and centered around a self-giving God who calls us to friendship through Christ and the Spirit. Put differently, the church is the community that lives from, in, and for the friendship of God that comes to us in Christ. If we see this

as our *vocation*, as the summons God extends to all of us, then
we know that in this friendship we are entrusted with the task
of being God's people in the world, of witnessing God's ways in
the world, and of furthering God's purposes in the world.

Learning the Language of God: How the Church Becomes the Community of the Friends of God

How then does our initiation into friendship with God begin?
Baptism is the primary sacrament of initiation and marks the
beginning of our formation in the Christian life, but the grammar of baptism is sustained and deepened as we learn the "language of God" through the worship and liturgy of the church.
In *What Ethics Is All About,* Herbert McCabe describes the Christian life as a community's endeavor to be initiated into and
formed according to the startling and scandalous language of
God that comes to us in the "Word" we call Jesus.[9] As McCabe
explains, Christianity begins in God's communication of a Word
to us. As the prologue to John's gospel articulates, "In the beginning was the Word." In the beginning God speaks, God delivers
a message, and the message has a name: Jesus, the *Logos,* the
Word of life. Every language is a matter of someone speaking
and others trying to respond. In Jesus, God speaks to us. Our
task is to hear the Word, to open our lives to receive it, and to
begin to live according to it. To take up the Christian life and to
be transformed from strangers to God into the friends of God,
we must allow the Word we call Jesus to become the guiding
grammar of our lives.

Jesus is the center of this new language because Jesus is not
only a revelation about God, he is also God's revelation about
ourselves. Jesus can be seen as a "Word" in two ways: he is the
self-communication of God to us, but he is also God's disclosure
of the meaning of our human lives and of our world. Jesus articulates God to us, but Jesus also reveals us to ourselves. When
we look to Jesus, we see who we most truthfully and promis-
ingly are. We see the kind of life that brings us to fullness. We
see the attitudes, values, practices, and behaviors that enable
human flourishing and happiness. More than anything, we see
the radical and redemptive truth we are called to live. In Jesus—

God's friendship to us *in person*—we fathom gracious truths about God and gracious truths about ourselves. This is why we can say Jesus is not only a person to follow, Jesus is also a *new language to learn.*

Thus, the Christian life of discipleship is the steadfast commitment to learn the language of God that comes to us in Christ and to strive to embody and witness it continually to the world. We are to speak to others in the language God has spoken to us; indeed, we are to become the Word that has been entrusted to us. But in order to witness to the Word of God, we must first become adept in its grammar. Our task is to move from being inarticulate with the Word to being eloquent practitioners of the Word.

This is not easy. As soon as we try to learn the language of God, we discover how different and difficult it is. God's language is unlike any we have tried to master before. It not only twists our tongues, it changes our hearts. In Jesus, God invites us to see life in a revolutionary new way. The divine language is so new and so different that when it is spoken in Jesus it sounds utterly strange to us—all this talk about forgiveness, turning the other cheek, being poor for the sake of the kingdom, and serving the needs of others before attending to our own. Not only do we fail to understand this language of God, we are also terribly threatened by it; as with Jesus' contemporaries, we find the language of God altogether too much for us (Matt. 13:57) and conclude its bearer must be "out of his mind" (Mark 3:21).

We cannot learn the language of God by measuring it against other languages and other ways of life. We can only learn this language if we realize it involves nothing less than dying to one understanding of life and taking up another. Jesus involves us in something qualitatively different, which is why we must see the Christian life of discipleship at its beginning as a fresh, clean start. As every disciple knows, following Jesus entails a break with the past and a reevaluation of everything we once considered important, the kind of radical reassessment echoed in Paul's famous boast in Philippians: "But those things I used to consider gain I have now reappraised as loss in the light of Christ. . . . For his sake I have forfeited everything; I have accounted all else rubbish so that Christ may be my wealth . . . (Phil. 3:7–8).

If we stay with the language of God, we recognize that we have crossed over to a new way of seeing, thinking, and behaving. In fact, the change is so momentous that the only way to capture it is to confess that in Christ we have become a new creation. Faithful to the language of God, we have become part of God's revolution, a revolution aptly named the reign of God. It is not so much a change of place as a change of person.

Learning the language of God implicates us in an ongoing transformation of how we think about everything. It explodes our sense of value and goodness and possibility because it takes its meaning from a God who calls us to question what we customarily accept and challenges us to embrace what we never before imagined. In Jesus, God speaks a different language, a wonderfully hopeful one because it is a language that affirms trust instead of betrayal, a language that seeks community instead of rivalry and division, a language that works for generosity instead of selfishness and domination, a language that values service more than privilege and gentleness more than self-promotion, and a language that practices forgiveness and peace because it knows the futility of vindictiveness and violence.

With the language of God, the center has shifted and a new age has begun, but it is not, oddly enough, an age of which we always want to be a part. We like to think we are faithful disciples and at one with Jesus, but for much of our lives Jesus can be more a scandal than a friend. One of the most confounding ironies of the Christian story is that God comes to offer us life and love, but we respond by putting God to death. We crucify the very one who is our hope. We say we want the life and hope Jesus brings, but when we have the chance to embrace it we turn away.

At least initially, and sometimes continually, we are scandalized by the ways of God. The world that so desperately needs the Word spurns the Word. As the cross starkly testifies, Jesus is the language we try to silence, the Word we put to death. We need the language of God, but we choose to remain with the language of death. In the shadow of the cross we see that God offers to reconstruct the world according to perfect love, but we kill such love because we fear it. As Herbert McCabe observes about the cross, "It is to say that this is the kind of world we have, a crucifying world, a world doomed to reject its own meaning."[10]

What might all this have to do with Christian worship? If my analysis is correct, it suggests we have to be apprenticed in the language of God in order to become the friends of God, and the primary place for this ongoing initiation to occur should be in the worship and liturgy of the church. To change from a person who crucifies the Word to a person who faithfully embodies the Word implies a drastic remaking of the self, and Christian worship should help us achieve this. If the Christian life is a matter of learning and appropriating the language of God, a language we first resist and work to destroy, then the Christian life involves the total reconstruction of the self from the deadly and ultimately futile ways of sin to the life-giving ways of God. This is what it means to be a disciple, a woman or man who learns from Jesus what a life of authentic friendship with God entails, and worship is the most fitting context for learning this. To be a disciple is to submit ourselves to being disciplined in the surprising and often confounding ways of God that come to us in Christ. We encounter those ways in worship and liturgy when we listen to the Word of God, open our lives to receive it, and learn from one another what it means to live that Word faithfully.

In worship we enter into a story that illumines the meaning and direction of our lives now. The saga of creation, fall, covenant, incarnation, redemption, and restoration is not a narrative we are to view from afar, but precisely the story that should govern our understanding of reality now and our sense of what being in the world involves. It is not so much that we bring our world to these stories of God we find in the Scriptures, but rather that we let these stories constitute, shape, and even remake our world. These are not incidents from a far off past to which we occasionally turn for inspiration, but the stories by which we want to know, understand, and live our lives now.

To be a Christian is to place our life in the center of a story of God we want to make our own. We do not inhabit this story passively; rather, we strive to appropriate it. We want to embody its viewpoints and perspectives; we wish its values and its vision to be our own. We want to grow so at home in the saga of Israel and Jesus that it gradually reformulates not only our reading of the world but also our understanding of ourselves.

It is through the constant rehearsal of the stories of God in worship that we learn to love and to live the language of God that is Jesus and therefore are gradually transformed in our new identity as the community of the friends of God. Worship puts us in touch with the formative memories of a people, but to remember liturgically is not simply to look back; rather, it is to bring the past to bear on the present in order to shape our lives a certain way. Remembering liturgically makes pivotal past events contemporaneous. Remembering liturgically is to recall and appropriate the stories, traditions, and practices we want to illumine, guide, and ultimately transform our lives.

More specifically, in Christian worship we pledge to live our lives in memory of Jesus, but that remembering is no abstract, intellectual exercise. To remember Jesus in worship is to make Jesus the one in whom and through whom we want to live now. What makes such worship poignant is that it releases Jesus from the confinement of the past so that he can live in and with us now—calling us from sin, challenging us and teaching us, leading us, and each day making us something new. In the worship and liturgy of the church, Christ becomes our contemporary, and we live as though we are his contemporaries—listening to him, conversing with him, learning from him, suffering with him, and rejoicing with him. Through the liturgy and worship of the church, Christ lives in us and we in him. Our life together is a friendship, a holy companionship with Christ. Thus, one day, much to our surprise, we find ourselves loving our enemies, forgiving those who have wronged us, serving others joyfully, and building one another up in love instead of using envy, jealousy, or resentment to tear one another down.

Thomas Aquinas captured the radical transformative effect liturgy and worship should have on the Christian community. In his writing about the Eucharist, he drew an analogy between food for our bodies and food for our souls. He said, "This sacrament does for the life of the spirit all that material food and drink does for the life of the body, by sustaining, building up, restoring, and contenting."[11] But there is a crucial difference between food for the body and food for the soul. When we eat a meal, Aquinas observed, the food we consume is digested and assimilated into our bodies to nourish and strengthen us. It is not we who are changed according to the food, but the food that is changed according to us. The spiritual food of the Eucharist is different. When we eat the body and drink the blood of Christ, it is not Christ who is changed according to us, but we who are changed according to Christ. As Aquinas puts it, "Spiritual food changes man into itself. This is the teaching of Augustine in his *Confessions*. He heard, as it were, the voice of Christ saying to him, 'You will not change me into yourself as you would the food of your flesh; but you will be changed into me.'"[12]

We become God's friends by "eating" Christ. We grow in friendship with God by feeding on the one who is the exemplar of that friendship. "So it is that as we were reborn in Christ through Baptism," Aquinas wrote, "we eat Christ through the Eucharist."[13] Aquinas does not flinch at this graphic description. He wants it to be clear that we acquire the self necessary for friendship with God by *eating* the life of Christ, by absorbing everything about him into our ordinary lives. When at the Eucharist we eat the body and drink the blood of Christ, we consume Christ entirely—his attitudes, his outlook, his values, his example—and we allow him to transform and to challenge our everyday lives. To feed on Christ in the Eucharist is to take Christ to heart; it is to allow Christ to affect every dimension of who we are. As Aquinas commented, food is of no use unless it is consumed, and the same is true with the food of Christ. It is of no use unless it is wholly consumed, completely taken to heart, so that our unredeemed life can be made over into his own.

Worship is central to a life of friendship with God because it works to achieve in us exactly the radical, total conformity of the self to Christ that is the perfection of friendship with God. It is through the worship and liturgy of the church that we become a person capable of intimacy and union with God, a person who wants nothing more than to give God glory and to honor God by following in the ways of his Son. Put differently, a life of friendship with God is centered in worship because it is there that we learn that our highest possible excellence is a life of being loved by God and loving God, a life of seeking God's good and delighting in God's beauty just as God seeks our good and delights in us. This is the language of friendship, and friendship with God is a life of shared intimacy and mutual indwelling, God living in us and we living in God through Christ.

Thus, Christian worship, if celebrated properly, should never be nostalgic consolation for us. Sham worship is nostalgia, and nostalgia is always sweet and always safe. Real worship is sometimes sweet but never safe because real worship releases Jesus from the past so that the full power of his person and his message can penetrate the present. For instance, when in the Gospels we see Jesus forgiving sins and setting people free, we are not to project that healing into an out-of-reach past. We are to ask how Jesus summons us to repentance and new life today, or how he challenges us to live a forgiven and forgiving way of life today. Christian worship is the summons to participate in the life of Christ *now* by developing in ourselves the dispositions, habits, and practices we see in Jesus. As Enda McDonagh wrote in *The Making of Disciples,* "In Christian liturgy, the primary events are the life, death and resurrection of the primary person, Jesus Christ, but not as an isolated person or remote past figure but as the fount and head of a people brought into being and continuously shaped by him and these events."[14] Or, as he said more pointedly, "Remembering in Christian liturgical terms is sharing. Person and events are not merely recalled but participated in."[15]

How Worshiping Dangerously Frees Us to Serve the World

If a life of friendship with God begins in and is centered in the liturgy and worship of the church, it is completed in mission. The worship and prayer of the church forms us into a special kind of community, but that community exists not for its own sake. It exists to share in and further the mission and ministry of Jesus. The friends of God are entrusted with the daunting mission of witnessing to the reign of God by striving to live according to it now. Without this extension of friendship with God into mission, such an understanding of the church risks being dangerously self-absorbed and elitist. A life of friendship with God should never turn the church away from the world; rather, it should instruct the church in precisely how it is called to serve the world. The friends of God are not an isolated elite but the community that recognizes the kind of people it needs to be if it is to live gratefully and generously the grace entrusted to it. Echoing Karl Barth's famous dictum, the friends of God do not flee or abandon the world, but sometimes are called to contradict it in ways that are full of hope.[16]

In *People of the Truth,* Clapp and Webber agree. They say the worship and prayer of the church should form the church into a "diacritical community." A diacritical community is one whose way of life often stands in contrast with the surrounding culture and society. A diacritical community, however, contradicts and challenges some of the values, customs, and practices of society not only to call attention to something that might be false and harmful but also to point to something much more graceful and promising. A diacritical community, such as the church is called to be, contradicts the world not for the sake of being odd or different but to call people's attention to a way of life that is undoubtedly challenging and demanding but also unabashedly joyful and full of hope. As Clapp and Webber explain, "The critic calls attention to something wrong; *the diacritic goes one step beyond criticism and distinguishes an alternative.* Accordingly, the church intends not only to criticize and contradict the identities and visions of the world, but to present a distinctive, alternative identity and vision."[17]

How then is the church, the *ecclesia* of the friends of God, called to serve the world in hope? If worship does not end when we leave the church building but is to continue and be completed in the witness of our lives, how should this happen? In general, worship should form a community of people who experience in Christ the freedom to live imaginatively and creatively. The friends of God ought to be a people so confident about the promises of God that they are willing to envision new possibilities, to be daring in their imitation of Christ, and even to have the courage to fail. So often what we find in churches is not daring and creative and imaginative, and there is certainly not enough confidence about the future to have the courage to fail, even joyfully, for the sake of the gospel. Rather, what we find is caution, timidity, small-mindedness, defensiveness, institutional paralysis, and too much concern about status, custom, and security to be willing to try anything new.

This is completely contrary to the witness and example of Christ. The portrait of Jesus presented in the Gospels shows him to be daring, imaginative, and amazingly creative in his efforts to institute and proclaim the reign of God. Jesus had no problem setting aside laws and traditions if he felt they were stifling the work of God and harming God's people. Part of Jesus' appeal was his freedom to be creative and his courage to be imaginative—so imaginative that he could envision a wholly new way of being human together. We see this creativity and imagination of Jesus at work in his ability to see more power in forgiveness than vindictiveness, in his belief that serving really is more liberating than being served, and in a love so imaginatively creative that it was willing to embrace all men and women as neighbors—even those neighbors who insist on being our enemies.

If churches today are willing to risk the "eschatological imagination"[18] of Jesus, if we are willing to live in the divine creativity of the reign of God, then, as Webber and Clapp suggest, we will "move from the 'destructively familiar to the creatively strange.'"[19] Do we trust the gospel enough to be creatively strange? Are we willing to be that imaginative, that hopeful, that prophetic a church for the sake of the world? What is the destructively familiar in our society, our cultures, our families and relationships, and even in our churches that needs to be confronted and overcome? Where are we summoned to be more imaginative and faithful as a church in order to serve better the world around us? These are the kinds of questions Christians ask when we start to worship dangerously and commit ourselves to being communities characterized not by lethargy or cynicism or timidity or divisiveness, but by the joy and hope and courage that ought to mark the friends of God.

What might this mean for Christian communities today? Many things suggest themselves, but two seem most urgent: nurturing and practicing the fruit of the Spirit that is love and nurturing and practicing the fruit of the Spirit that is peace.[20]

First then, what about love? Love doesn't sound so dangerous until you've tried it, especially if you try to imitate the costly love of Christ. Liturgy and worship should form us into the kind of Christian community we see in the writings of Paul. If you scan the letters of Paul in the New Testament, you find him constantly describing the kind of attitudes, dispositions, and practices Christians ought to show one another in their life together. He says Christians are to honor one another (Rom. 12:10), live in harmony with one another (Rom. 12:18), accept one another (Rom. 15:7), care for one another (1 Cor. 12:25), be servants of one another (Gal. 5:13), bear one another's burdens (Gal. 6:2), comfort one another (1 Thess. 5:11), be at peace with one another (1 Thess. 5:13), bear with one another lovingly (Eph. 4:2), and forgive one another (Col. 3:13).[21]

All of these are concrete practices of love—they show us what love actually looks like. We practice love when we honor one another, when we try to live in harmony with one another, when we care for one another, when we are kind to one another, serve one another, bear with each other patiently, comfort one another, forgive one another, and are not afraid to challenge one another and speak the truth to one another. Each of these things is a practice of love, and all of them should be formed in us through worship.

Taken together, these concrete practices of love can be summarized by Paul's term of "building one another up." Isn't that what love ultimately involves? Isn't love a matter of building each other up through support, encouragement, care, respect, truthfulness, and consolation? Doesn't it mean so much to us when someone takes a moment to encourage us, affirm us, or simply give us attention? Who in our lives now needs building up? Who right before us today needs encouragement and support?

Isn't love the kind of active commitment we have for one another when each day we seek what is best for each other, when each day we devote our energies and attention to the needs and well-being of others and find joy in doing so? Is this the kind of community and people our worship is making of us? When we leave worship, do we build one another up in love? Do we look for ways to honor one another? Are we consistently truthful with each other?

It sounds simple and so appealing, but what makes the practices of love difficult is that we easily become experts not at building one another up but at tearing one another to pieces. Think of how easy it is to gossip, to spread rumors about others, to be cynical. It is always easier to tear down than to build up because building one another up in truth and in love requires much more commitment, much more imagination, much more patience, and certainly much more generosity. This is the sort of dangerous love worship should be forming in us if we are truly living in friendship with God. This is how we are called to move from the destructively familiar to embrace the creatively strange we see so hopefully witnessed in Jesus and his message of the reign of God.

It is equally clear that the fruits of Jesus' costly love are meant not only for our immediate families, communities, or relationships. Jesus goes further. Jesus says we are to risk the kind of love that makes us unafraid to love our neighbor no matter who that neighbor might be.

This sounds strange. Why would anyone be afraid to love his neighbor? Because it all depends on who the neighbor is. It is easy enough to love our neighbor if we are allowed to limit and control who our neighbor is. It is easy to love our neighbor if the only ones we allow to fall under that welcoming title are people we like, admire, or enjoy being with.

This is "safe neighbor love," and all of us are good at it. Safe neighbor love is choosy. It zeroes in on people who are rather easy to love. Safe neighbor love is easy to practice because it allows us to reach out to those we want to love but exclude those we find difficult to love.

The trouble with safe neighbor love is that it makes our world too small. With safe neighbor love we draw the boundary of love too tight, shutting out those we may find difficult to love, letting in only those who are rather easy to love. Safe neighbor love operates on the rhythm of exclusion and embrace—we reject some, we accept others. This may be normal enough and perhaps even understandable, but it is all too destructively familiar to have the power truly to bring new life to our world. It is not nearly creatively strange enough to share in the love Jesus calls us to practice for the sake of the kingdom of God.

Safe neighbor love too easily assumes that not everybody counts, that large groups of people are expendable and don't really matter because of some difference in them we find disturbing, whether it be the color of their skin, their ethnic background, their sexual orientation, their religion, their politics, their physical and mental qualities, or even their ecclesiastical status. Embracing some but excluding others is the way of safe neighbor love but is totally opposed to the risky and radical love we see living in Christ.[22]

Nobody understood this better than Dorothy Day, activist and cofounder of the Catholic Worker Movement, who devoted her life to serving the most marginalized members of society. Day was able to move beyond the destructively familiar of safe neighbor love and commit herself to befriending exactly the people most of us find most difficult to love: the poor, the homeless, the unemployed, all those whose lives have failed by conventional canons of success. Dorothy Day embraced the very ones our world finds it so easy to exclude because she *worked* at seeing Christ in them and believed that even when she could not see Christ in another, he was there. She saw the poor as gifts to receive, not as nuisances to deplore. She was able to practice this risky and costly love because through worship and prayer she learned what it means to live in friendship with God. Day began each day by going to Mass, and as she notes in her autobiography, *The Long Loneliness,* she never would have learned what it means to love like Christ had she not first learned what it means to praise and give thanks. Her expertise in love and justice was cultivated and nurtured through the Eucharist; it grew from the worship and prayer of her life.[23]

There is nothing at all easy about imitating Christ's love because the Gospels make it clear that Jesus *excludes no one.* Throughout the Gospels, Jesus reaches out to all those our social, economic, political, and even religious institutions work so hard to exclude. We see him time and time again embracing the excluded ones as he sits down at the table with prostitutes, tax collectors, lawbreakers, and all kinds of sinners.

Practicing this kind of love of neighbor is risky. Indeed, it is the most radical and demanding love of all because it means we are to love whomever God loves and love them because God loves them. The fellowship formed by God's love is no small community. It is the one community where there is room for everybody because *God embraces, God never excludes,* and this is what the worship and liturgy of the church should teach us, the kind of love it should form in us, and the sort of people it should make of us. What does this say to the contemporary sins of racism and sexism? To our numbing indifference to the poor? How might it challenge our attitudes to persons with AIDS? To those we are comfortable dismissing? How does it challenge our churches when sometimes they are much better at excluding and dismissing than welcoming and embracing, especially excluding the people whose lives don't quite conform to the niceties of ecclesiastical law?

We are called in the Eucharist, in liturgy, and in worship to practice a love that never excludes and always embraces. This is what makes authentic worship so dangerous in a world that is built on principles of exclusion. Indeed, ours is a world that *thrives* on exclusion and encourages us to gain our identity by dominating or dismissing somebody else. That is not the way of Christ, who broke open the boundaries of community so that there would be no difference between insider and outsider, between the excluded and the embraced, and called this new community formed by ever expansive love the kingdom of God.

One of the most important ways we can imitate Christ in our world today and move from the destructively familiar to the creatively strange is to love all our neighbors each day, no matter who the neighbor is who crosses our path. This can sound banal, but there really is no more morally charged act than to love our neighbor because, as Rosa comments in Tennessee Williams's play *The Rose Tattoo,* "Everybody is nothing until you love them!"[24]

All of us know this to be true. Not to love our neighbor is to make them nothing, to steal away their identity. Not to pay attention to them is to say they do not matter, to make them disappear.

To love another person is, like God, to draw them to life and to gift them with identity and significance. To love another person is to see the image of God in them—that unique spark of God entrusted to them—and affirm it. To love is to *pay attention to the other.* It is to attend to the needs, concerns, interests, and well-being of another, whether that other be spouse, child, fellow community member, student, stranger, or friend. When we pay attention to the other—when we embrace rather than exclude—we bring the other to life. There is a scene in *The Rose Tattoo* that captures this. Rosa tells Jack:

> And a few minutes later you said to me, "Gee, you're beautiful!" I said, "Excuse me," and ran to the ladies' room. Do you know why? To look at myself in the mirror! And I saw that I was! For the first time in my life I was beautiful! You'd made me beautiful when you *said* that I was![25]

That's Christian neighbor love. There is no more powerful act than to love our neighbor, because when we do, we become the mirror in which they see themselves as beautiful. Through our love, kindness, thoughtfulness, patience, and consideration, we reflect back to them a beauty, dignity, and sacredness they otherwise might not see or even know they have. This is the love the church, the community of the friends of God, is challenged to practice, and it is the love our prayer and worship should be nurturing in us.

The Friends of God as a People of Peace

A second way the church is called to live in the divine creativity of the reign of God is to nurture and practice the fruit of the Spirit that is peace. Christian worship should make us a *peacemaking people of a peacemaking God*. Indeed, one of the most significant contributions Christians as the friends of God can make in our world today is to show that people can live together in peace.

In their 1983 pastoral letter *The Challenge of Peace*, the Catholic bishops of the United States stressed that "Peacemaking is not an optional commitment. It is a requirement of our faith. We are called to be peacemakers, not by some movement of the moment, but by our Lord Jesus."[26] Being peacemakers is part of what it means to live a gospel life. Being peacemakers is essential to the vocation of living in friendship with God. We are called to be a people of peace, a people whose lives together show that division and brokenness and rivalry and violence are not inevitable.

In their pastoral letter, the bishops said every follower of Christ is challenged "to live up to the call of Jesus to be peacemakers in our own time and situation."[27] What would this mean for us in our families? In our workplaces? In all of our relationships? In our churches? Where are we called to be *instruments of a peacemaking God* in our lives right now? Where are we called to work for healing and reconciliation instead of allowing brokenness to prevail?

In Ephesians 2:13–22, Paul speaks of Christ and his cross breaking down the walls that divide us. He speaks of Christ removing all the barriers that keep us apart and overcoming the hostilities that so often leave us living more at enmity with one another than in peace. It is a powerful image because it presumes those walls and barriers are there but also affirms that they need not prevail. What are the walls that divide people in our world today? Where might there be obstacles to reconciliation and peace in our own lives?

There is no shortage of barriers that need to be dismantled if God's dream of peace and well-being for all is to become a reality. We create barriers through our attitudes toward others. We create barriers when we freeze other people out or simply ignore them. We create barriers when we refuse to talk to certain people and find all kinds of ways to exclude them. We create barriers when we refuse to deal with the problems that weaken relationships. We create barriers when we refuse to give ourselves to others. We create barriers when we hold on to grudges and refuse to forgive. We create barriers when we nurture anger, cynicism, bitterness, and resentment instead of seeking peace.

Listen again to the words of Ephesians. In Ephesians 4:31–32, Paul tells the Christian community to "get rid of all bitterness, all passion and anger, harsh words, slander, and malice of every kind." Paul says leave all that behind, get away from it, and refuse to be ruled by it because all those things put walls and barriers between ourselves and others. Instead, Paul says, "be kind to one another, compassionate, and mutually forgiving, just as God has forgiven you in Christ." These are the practices of peace. We nurture peace among ourselves and others when we are people marked by kindness, compassion, healing, reconciliation, and forgiveness.

What is Paul telling us? He is saying, "Remember how God has been to you, then go and do likewise to one another. Be a reconciling presence in the world. Be imitators of the God who forgives and befriends and seeks peace." Paul's point is that the fundamental ministry of God in Christ is a ministry of befriending reconciliation and peace, and we are called to embody this ministry every day of our lives.

One of the greatest contributions the church can make today is to be this befriending community, to be a people who live by the power of forgiveness, reconciliation, and peace. There is a passage in Paul's second letter to the church at Corinth (2 Cor. 5:18–20) that says just this. There Paul says God "has entrusted a ministry of reconciliation to us." The image is of God hand-ing on to us the ministry of reconciliation begun on the cross. What Paul suggests is that whether or not God's ministry of reconciliation and peace continues depends on us. God needs a community; God needs a people in the world committed to live not by the sickly powers of rivalry and divisiveness but by the life-giving powers of forgiveness, reconciliation, and peace.

If we pledged ourselves to be a peacemaking people of a peacemaking God, what would this mean? At the very least, it would mean we promise to be a people who refuse to pass on the hurt. It would mean that we promise to be a people who refuse to pass on whatever harm, slight, or injustice we suffer. This is a choice we have every day. When we are hurt we can pass on the hurt, adding to the barriers between us and others, or we can look for ways to take those barriers down. When we are wounded by another's thoughtlessness or malice, we can respond by seeking revenge or we can practice something much more creative and hopeful: we can practice the fruit of the Spirit that is peace.

Of course, the practice of the love and peace of Christ cannot be achieved alone. This understanding of the church and the Christian life requires companions committed to the same adventure of faith to which we have committed ourselves. If the church is to be a community of friends joined together in Christ, it is important that we understand precisely what such friendships are, what they require, and the irreplaceable contribution they make to our life in Christ. These are matters we shall explore in the next four chapters.

two

Exploring the Mysteries of Intimacy

What Hinders and What Helps the Friendships of Our Lives

One of the most beautiful movies of recent years told a story of friendship. The movie is *Shadowlands*, the story of the marriage of C. S. Lewis, the famous English author and philosopher, to Joy Gresham, an American poet. Lewis did not marry Joy until late in life. For years he had been, and fully expected to remain, an inveterate bachelor. He liked the bachelor's life, its cozy routines, its comfort and predictability.

But then Joy rushed in and his life was never quite the same. Their marriage lasted only a short time because Joy falls ill with cancer and dies, but in the few years they had together, Joy Gresham changed C. S. Lewis's life in surprising, unexpected ways. She drew him out of himself. She taught him lessons in trust and caring and openness. She educated him in those deep mysteries of love, suffering, loss, and hope.

C. S. Lewis and Joy Gresham were husband and wife, but they were also one another's best friends. Like all good friends, they loved one another and they loved being together. They enjoyed the small but important pleasures of life together, pleasures such as a good conversation, making each other laugh, teasing one another, or simply going through a day together. Like all good friends, they shared important things in common—values and ideals, deep cares and concerns, a kindred vision of life. As best friends always do, they made one another better as they helped each other grow in goodness, holiness, and love. It is no surprise then to hear C. S. Lewis say to Joy one day, "You were alive before. I wasn't. . . . I started living when I started loving you, Joy. That makes me only a few months old."[1]

Friendship is one of the greatest gifts of life; without friendship our lives would be impossibly impoverished. We can appreciate the great significance of friendship when we think how different our lives would be if certain people had never entered into them. Not only would our history be different, but we would be different as well. Our friends shape our character. They influence our attitudes, values, and perceptions. They challenge us, they teach us not to take ourselves too seriously, and they give us hope.

Most important, friends want what is best for us and help us achieve it. They see our most promising possibilities—the true image of God in us—and help shape that image to completion. As the story of Joy Gresham and C. S. Lewis illustrates so beautifully, our best friends help us to be our best selves, which is why we are always better for having spent time with them. It is in company with these good friends that we come to understand better what life means for us, the kind of person we ought to become, and what will really make us happy and free. Good friends not only change us, they make us better persons. Is it any wonder Aristotle said, "Without friendships no one would choose to live, even if they had all other good things in life."[2]

Friendship is an art. All of us have a natural need for friends, but none of us naturally knows what it means to be a friend. Being a good friend requires being a certain kind of person, a person of certain character, attitudes, virtues, and dispositions. We cannot presume everyone has a solid understanding of what good and healthy friendships require or that they have the dispositions and skills necessary for being a good friend. Some people call friendships relationships that are not friendships at all; they are manipulative, abusive relationships. I had a student once who wrote an essay on friendship. I remember that essay because of one unforgettable passage: "My boyfriend is my best friend. He always tells me when I am wrong." Is that a good friendship? Will she find there the love, care, and concern that will help her be her best self and know happiness?

We live in a culture that misunderstands, trivializes, and often subverts friendship. Perhaps our culture even fears good friendships because one of the gifts of friendship is to free us to see and think and live differently by imagining better and healthier possibilities for ourselves. In so many ways our culture trains us to be unfit for friendship. For instance, how can we sustain good friendships when our culture encourages us to use others, claiming them as friends when they are advantageous but abandoning them when they are not? How can we nurture lasting friendships in a society that idolizes busyness and constant activity, preaching to us that the best life is the life lived "on the run"? What happens to friendships in a society that teaches us that freedom requires being unobliged and uncommitted, when we know one thing friends do is oblige and limit us precisely because friendship is a commitment of availability to another?

Friendship with God is lived through friendship with others, but friendship, a most necessary relationship, is also a distinctive and special relationship that requires certain kinds of persons. How do people understand friendship today? What have been their models for friendships or their experience with relationships? Does everyone have the emotional, psychological, and spiritual maturity necessary for friendship? These are the questions we shall ponder in this chapter as we explore both the graces and the challenges of friendship.

Obstacles and Impediments to Friendship

Perhaps the greatest human need is a need for intimacy. Yes, to survive physically we need food, shelter, and clothing, but to survive spiritually and emotionally we need intimacy. The story of the creation of man and woman in Genesis suggests no less. God's original insight into our human condition is that it is not good for us to be alone. We need companionship and partnership with others if our souls are not to shrivel. As Elizabeth Achtemeier observed, God's declaration that it is not good for us to be alone is the first of many "merciful words" God speaks to humanity. It is telling that the first merciful word from God concerns our need for human intimacy and companionship; that this insight comes at the dawn of our creation suggests from the very beginning we stand in absolute need of another.[3]

Have we structured and shaped our lives together in a way that honors the wisdom of God's insight? Have we not in so many ways constructed a world that not only makes genuine intimacy difficult but also seems actively to work against it? In *The Search for Intimacy*, Elaine Storkey says, "the conditions in which real intimacy can develop and grow seem to be increasingly absent in the world we inhabit."[4] Indeed, "far from enhancing the possibility of intimacy," she writes, "the very way in which society has been structured seems to put people at a distance from each other."[5]

Despite God's merciful word and our inherent need for friendship and intimacy, in many respects we seem much better at loneliness than we are at intimacy. It is a disturbing idea but a hard one to avoid when we consider how many people are captive to loneliness, the pain of broken relationships, or a cynicism about the possibility of any real and lasting love. Have we sabotaged our happiness by becoming more adept at isolation and loneliness than we are at intimacy and friendship? Is it true that we have learned best how to be strangers to one another—even to the people with whom we live everyday—but that this has happened so quietly and gradually we hardly realize how disconnected we have become?

If we took a snapshot of ordinary everyday life, we would see lots of people in a hurry, people rushing past one another but not really paying attention to one another. We would see people who go through day after day, week after week, never really sharing anything that matters with another, never truly sharing their thoughts, feelings, fears, joys, or concerns. We would see, sadly, too many families who live under the same roof but remain private individuals apart, more like cordial strangers than family members. We would see marriages in which spouses long ago stopped trying to communicate with one another and who allow television to be the emotional tether between them. We would see far too many who long ago gave up on human intimacy and retreat to their rooms to find solace on the Internet. How did all this happen?

First, where we live and how we live has changed in ways that are not always healthy for friendship and intimacy. It has become commonplace to claim that many Americans have little sense of the importance of geographical rootedness. Fewer and fewer of us have any real experience of what it is to live in a true neighborhood. Many of us have no idea who our neighbors are because our day-to-day life takes us away from our homes. We work outside our neighborhoods, shop outside our neighborhoods, play outside our neighborhoods. Our neighbors are strangers who happen to live next door.

There is little need to know them, sometimes little opportunity. For instance, for all the benefits of air conditioning, it does keep us apart from those who live nearby. Fewer of us keep our windows open in the summer where we could actually hear our neighbors, or sit on porches where we might talk with them and begin to know them. Even more, the increased mobility of our society may have given us the freedom to go where we want when we want, but it also uproots us and works against the stability necessary for relationships to begin and to grow. Developing friendships demands that at least occasionally we slow down and stay put, but hardly anyone today stays in the same place for very long. Instead of putting down roots, we are accustomed to being uprooted by our jobs, by the need for bigger and better homes, or simply because of our desire for something new and different. All of this is hard on friendships because friendships require people who are able to slow down long enough to get to know one another, who can be available to one another long enough for friendship to take root and grow. Increased mobility and uprootedness can create psychological and emotional impediments to friendships because we are less likely to invest in relationships if we think either we or a potential friend will not be around long enough to enjoy them.

As mentioned above, the pastimes of our everyday lives can leave the most important relationships of our lives malnourished. For example, the popularity of fast-food restaurants means fewer families have dinner at home. Even when families do eat at home, seldom are all family members present because of conflicting schedules and multiple activities, many of them good (sports teams, service activities, choir practice), but each of them contributing to a situation where the time and space necessary for families to be together, to form bonds of intimacy, and to know one another *as a family* vanish. How many families do we know who may be at the table together, but whose attention is directed at a television instead of one another? We tire of hearing how television and computers have contributed to our increased isolation from one another, but we are so transfixed by them we seldom consider how they rob us of what we most need and secretly want, namely, a way of being that would allow us to be truly present to another. Exchanging quips and comments during commercials won't achieve this.

Second, friendships are imperiled by the haughty individualism of our culture. We live in a society that teaches us to put ourselves and our needs before the needs and well-being of others. Even our moral vocabulary reflects this. Gone is the language of the common good. In its place is the language of individual rights, personal choice, and privacy. These things are important, but a person whose primary concern is individual rights and his personal well-being is a poor candidate for friendship. The very qualities requisite for friendship, qualities such as generosity and thoughtfulness, are hardly nurtured in a society that tells us we must look after ourselves first because nobody else will.

Radical individualism is such a powerful cultural ideology that even when we question it we are not sure how to work against it. Such an understanding of the self sees us not primarily as social and relational beings who need others in order to develop and flourish but as essentially private, solitary, and autonomous individuals for whom relationships are more likely an unwanted restriction than the key to our humanization. Moreover, when our culture gives "unqualified public approval to the drive for individual success, individual affluence and individual profit,"[6] other people are more likely to be seen as rivals and competitors than friends.

This is foolish. The irony of individualism is that while it promises happiness and success, it dead-ends in a very lonely, empty life. None of us can make ourselves happy. None of us is the answer to life's incompleteness and hunger for meaning. We are taught by our society to "seek our privacy and freedom with a passion, not wanting any interdependence forced upon us," Elaine Storkey explains. "We seek our own private life, with a private house, a private car, a private office, and not content with that, we want within our home a private room, a private telephone, a private television and so on." But "once we have attained that, and systematically undercut many of our interdependencies with other people, then we wonder why we are lonely."[7]

Individualism dead-ends in loneliness because human beings are inherently and inescapably social beings who need to live in deep, intimate, enriching relationships with others. Our psychological, emotional, spiritual, and even physical well-being depends on us living in relationship with others. Put even more strongly, we can have neither a self nor an identity in any truly human and personal sense apart from a variety of relationships marked by care, affection, affirmation, and faithfulness. This is why the Scottish philosopher John Macmurray stressed that we realize ourselves as persons not by withdrawing from the sometimes messy complexities of relationships but only through "the full mutuality of fellowship in a common life."[8]

For Macmurray, the basic unit of personal existence is not the autonomous individual who prizes privacy above all else, "but two persons in personal relation."[9] We are not fully formed individuals for whom intimate relationships are arbitrary possibilities; rather, we grow into true individuality and personhood only in and through relationships with others. As Macmurray says, "The unit of the personal is not the 'I', but the "You and I.'"[10]

We grow as human beings through relationships that draw us out of ourselves, give us life, teach us how to love, and lead to deepening communion. As Emmanuel Mounier writes, "the *we* . . . is prior to the *I*" because selfhood does not preexist our relationships, but is made possible by them. "One might almost say," Mounier continues, "that I have no existence, save in so far as I exist for others, and that to be is, in the final analysis, to love."[11] It is because of this that the desire to be in communion with others, no matter how steadfastly we may repress or avoid it, remains the most fundamental spiritual inclination of our nature.

To be human is to be possessed by the aching need to give our self to others and to receive the gift of another's self in return.

This indeed is the heart of friendship. An undying need of every human being is the need to *communicate our self,* to share our soul and spirit with others in the hope that we might live in communion with them. This reciprocal communication of selves is the most humanizing and life-giving activity, and it is the lifeblood of friendship—whether it be friendship with God, the special friendship of marriage, or friendship with others.

We can appreciate this if we consider what happens to people who never learn to love, people who never develop a capacity to share, or people who must always be in control. Similarly, we can appreciate our keen need for others when we reflect on the destiny of people who are controlled by fear, anger, bitterness, anxiety, cynicism, or resentment. As trite as it may sound, they *cannot possibly be happy* because they are deprived of the very relationships that make happiness possible. Happiness requires befriending others and being befriended by them. It demands *shared existence.* This is why people who never learn what it means to love or who have never been loved are emotionally, morally, and spiritually dead.

A third obstacle to intimacy and friendship is our culture's increasingly economic understanding of life. In many respects capitalism has grown to be not only our economic system but also our culture's master narrative.[12] It shapes our view of the world, our understanding of ourselves, and certainly our sense of what matters and counts for success. It teaches us what to value and care about, what we should desire, and it guides our understanding of happiness and fulfillment. We live in a society where increasingly almost everything is seen in market categories, and anything, including ourselves, can be a commodity. In Western society today the fundamental value of anything is determined economically. How does this effect relationships? Do we value friendship less because it has no cash value? Is family life no longer worthy because when we devote time to our spouses and children we are not being economically productive?

Years ago, the Trappist monk, author, and social critic Thomas Merton wrote an essay titled "Love and Need: Is Love a Package or a Message?" Merton argued that the language and categories of a market economy have so permeated our culture, including our understanding of relationships, that we think of "ourselves and others not as *persons* but as *products*."[13] Love becomes a form of salesmanship in which we must make ourselves an attractive "product" so that another person might "invest" in us. Love is a matter of trying to "sell ourselves" to others by finding a way not only to make ourselves desirable to them but also wanted and needed by them. As Merton said, "We unconsciously think of ourselves as objects for sale on the market. We want to be wanted. We want to attract customers."[14] Lest this sound farfetched, look at the personal or dating ads in any newspaper. There you will find pages of names of persons, each trying to make his or her self desirable to another but doing so in the sparse, abbreviated language of the classifieds. Think about what we tell college seniors when we prepare them for the harsh world of the "job market." They are told they must learn how to "market" themselves and find ways to make themselves an attractive "product" for a potential employer.

We live in a culture that is aggressively materialistic, a culture that urges us to believe we need things more than we need people. This is part of our cultural creed. Consumerism is a gospel, and it tells us we are liberated through what we own, not through intimate relationships, and that our identity is measured by our possessions, not by the richness of our loves. As Storkey says, we confuse "affluence with emotional satisfaction, material well-being with intimacy."[15]

Consumerism is a theory of investments. It teaches us to invest in things rather than persons because money and possessions will fulfill us in ways no person can. It tells us to find our security in wealth and property because they cannot betray us like our friends can. In a consumeristic society, friends are just another commodity, something to be bought, used, and disposed of as we see fit. In consumerism, a friend is another novelty that is quickly and easily replaced when something new and more interesting comes along. "Instead of being taught to love people and use things," Storkey observes, "we are more often taught to love things and use people."[16]

Consumerism and materialism are lethal for friendships because good and lasting friendships are possible only with people who are able to be content and satisfied with other people, but the last thing our consumerist culture wants is for us to be content with anything, even one another. Quite the opposite, consumerism fosters discontent. It encourages us to be chronically restless and dissatisfied so that we will always want more and buy more. The message of our economic system is that it is foolish to rest content with anything, even another person. We should always be seeking something more fulfilling, satisfying, and exciting.[17]

Similarly, consumerism teaches us that nothing lasts, including relationships. If a product wears out or breaks down, we don't repair it; we throw it away and buy a new one. We are conditioned to think that eventually everything grows obsolete. How does this effect our relationships, especially our capacity to make commitments and to remain faithful? Do people today really expect relationships to last? Are we not conditioned to expect them to grow stale or to fall apart? An essential virtue for any lasting relationship is faithfulness, but faithfulness implies a commitment to do everything possible to keep our relationships vital and strong and to renew them when they are not. A good friendship is not one that never knows struggles or never grows stale, but one in which the friends do not abandon one another when it does.

So we see that consumerism and materialism undermine friendships and intimate relationships for two primary reasons. First, they seriously misunderstand what a good friendship is. In the ideology of consumerism, the primary purpose of any relationship is to fulfill our needs, but this fundamentally redefines what a friendship is. No one would deny that good friendships ought to be satisfying and meaningful and thus fulfill needs, but the principal aim of friendship is not the fulfillment of our needs. Caring for the good and well-being of another is. Our needs may often be fulfilled in friendship, but they aren't always, and even when they are it is only indirectly. If we enter into a relationship with the avowed purpose of fulfilling our needs, that relationship is doomed because we will use and manipulate another for our purposes. Need fulfillment may be a result of a good friendship, but it surely is not its purpose. Traditionally, anyone who said the basic purpose of friendship was to satisfy one's needs would not have understood friendship and would be a very poor candidate for a friend. The distinctive mark of any friendship is to be a part of a relationship where our energy and attention is devoted to the good of the other, not ourselves.

Second, consumerism and materialism undermine intimacy and friendship because they form in people qualities of character that are the antithesis of what good friendship requires. Good friendship requires persons who are fundamentally just, who are of generous spirit, who are loyal, faithful, and trustworthy, and who are willing to make themselves present and available to others. If we believe what we own matters more than who we love, we will hardly be unselfish enough to seek the good of another for her or his own sake or find joy in expending ourselves for their well-being, which is exactly what friendships require. If we have never been taught to rest content with anything, we will not be able to sustain the commitment, presence, and faithfulness real intimacy demands.

Character Traits That Are Obstacles to Friendship

Intimate friendships are not only jeopardized by certain elements of our culture and lifestyles, they can also be weakened and even destroyed by qualities of our personality and character. For instance, Elaine Storkey speaks of "overdetachment" as a serious obstacle to intimacy and friendship.[18] A person who is overdetached has difficulty getting close to anyone. He or she so values independence and privacy that as soon as another person draws close to them they pull back. People who are overdetached may have several relationships, but those relationships tend to be superficial, more acquaintances than intimate relationships. Moreover, people who are overly detached and distant can appear quite friendly and congenial, masters of charm and subtle humor. In reality, they are masters of evasiveness who have learned well all the strategies of avoidance. People who are overly detached abhor the demands of intimacy, especially the vulnerability and truthfulness inherent in any intimate relationship, as well as the time, presence, and availability such relationships entail. These people need to be in control, and the last thing they want is to be beholden to others in any way that would tie them down or hold them accountable.

Overdetachment is a serious character flaw that cripples any possibility for intimacy. It can also be a source of grievous injustice in relationships such as marriage and even religious community life where affection, intimacy, and openness are owed another. One of the saddest, but unfortunately not uncommon, spectacles is the marriage where one partner is overly detached and remote but the other desires a real sharing of life. The overly detached spouse sees nothing wrong with the relationship and cannot understand the other's unease. He or she has no need for sharing, conversation, and intimacy and is puzzled by the other's unhappiness.

Sadly, such spouses can live together for years but share very little between them. A pattern of not relating is established. When communication occurs, it focuses on the trivial, the safe, and the predictable. Instead of conversation there is chitchat. Nothing from the heart, nothing truly personal is ever shared. Eventually, what is meant to be an intimate relationship and a true communion of life becomes nothing more than two very detached strangers who happen to live under the same roof.

Even though overdetached people can appear jovial and approachable, they lack a sense of playfulness and humor precisely because playfulness can be so self-revealing and vulnerable. Indeed, playfulness almost always involves some loss of control, the very thing the overly detached most fear. In reality, humor and playfulness are usually signs of a healthy, strong relationship. Playfulness is a sign not only that people are comfortable with one another but also that they are not afraid to be themselves with one another. Playfulness allows the masks and facades to melt away and a kind of "epiphany in silliness" to occur where people reveal themselves more honestly and completely to another. Along with cynicism and bitterness, overdetachment is toxic for the soul and deadly for intimate relationships such as marriage and friendship. The harvest of overdetachment is not freedom and independence or heightened productivity but a lonely and ultimately emotionally impoverished life.

The opposite of overdetachment, but equally perilous for intimacy and friendship, is overattachment or possessiveness. Possessive persons are so driven by a need for intimacy and closeness that they suffocate the persons they claim to love. In the name of love they always want to be together with the persons they love, but such love soon becomes a prison for the beloved. True intimacy demands not only knowing how to be together but also knowing when and how to be apart. Intimacy demands giving one another sufficient time and space to be by themselves *for the sake of the relationship*, but this is exactly what overly possessive persons are afraid to risk. They are so insecure in their relationships that they believe that if they let the other person out of their sight they will lose her because she will surely find someone else more lovable and appealing. What claims to be a relationship of deep love becomes excessively controlling and manipulative.

There may be many reasons for overattachment. Often it can be traced to a lack of self-esteem or self-confidence rooted in the conviction that one is not very lovable or desirable. Possessiveness grows from insecurity, from fear and anxiety, from past experiences of betrayal or infidelity, and from the pain of having lost a beloved. All of this may make possessiveness understandable, but it has to be overcome if a relationship is to be healthy and lasting. Real intimacy should be freeing, but possessive relationships fear freedom. Real intimacy is built on trust and openness and respect, but possessive relationships are inevitably characterized by jealousy and insecurity because the supposed beloved becomes completely subordinate to the unquenchable needs of the other.

Obviously, possessiveness dooms friendship and intimacy—or else guarantees a very unhealthy relationship—because there is no way anyone can fulfill the emotional, psychological, and affective needs of the possessive person nor eliminate his or her insecurities. No matter how much attention, affection, and love you extend to such persons, they never feel secure; consequently, the person trying to assure them of their lovableness feels defeated and exhausted.

Intimacy and the Power of the Past

Finally, intimacy and friendship can be effected by the power of the past. All of us are shaped by our past for better or worse, and we bring the influence of that past with us to every relationship. We may not be fully determined by our past, but we surely are products of our past, whether it be our family history or our past relationships. For instance, there is the common saying that every husband and wife brings their parents' marriage with them into their own marriage. Similarly, anyone who has experienced betrayal, deception, or abandonment in a relationship is haunted by those sorrowful memories when they enter new relationships. They may desperately want to overcome the lingering effects of those experiences, but healing takes time.

Tragically, a growing number of persons, especially women, have been victims of violence, sometimes even from persons who claimed to love them. Violence, particularly the violence of rape or sexual abuse, effects a person not only physically but psychologically, emotionally, and spiritually because it is an attack on the soul and spirit of a person, not just his or her body. Such awful experiences become part of what the theologian H. Richard Niebuhr called a person's "inner history."[19] Inner history refers to the experiences and events that have a profoundly formative and lasting effect on us. Even though they may have happened long ago, they live on in us and continue to shape us.

One of the graces of good friendship is to help people deal with the wounds and brokenness of their lives through the steadfast love and care of another. Part of the realism of good friendship is knowing the wounds and brokenness are there and must be dealt with lest a person's life shuts down in fear, hurt, anger, resentment, and bitterness. All those things are normal and even healthy reactions to betrayal, deceit, or violence, but they must gradually be overcome if they are not to be the overriding story of a person's life.

Friendship, Intimacy, and the Role of the Church

This lengthy chronicle of the barriers to intimacy and friendship can sound so distressing that we despair of the possibilities of genuine friendship at all. The challenges to intimacy and friendship should not defeat us, but they should be sobering enough to make us realize we cannot assume that everyone either understands or has a capacity for healthy, intimate relationships. In many respects, I think, friendship and intimacy have become endangered species in our culture. If so, is there a "habitat" or setting that can provide the proper environment or "ecology" for the preservation of true intimacy and friendship?[20] I think there is—or at least should be—in the church. If the church is faithful to its identity as the friends of God, it should be a befriending community that not only welcomes all who come to it but also offers them a place where the grammar of intimacy and friendship can be learned. Moreover, if authentic friendship is an endangered species in our society, then an urgent ministry of the church today may be to help create a supportive environment where true friendship and rich intimacy can be witnessed, embodied, and experienced.

John Kavanaugh makes a similar suggestion in his *Still Following Christ in a Consumer Society*. As an alternative to the debilitating effects of the consumerism of our culture, Kavanaugh says Christian churches must promote and embody the "Personal Form" of life. The "Personal Form" of life is characterized first by recognition of the absolute uniqueness and irreplaceable dignity of every individual and, second, by the belief that every human being is called to a covenant relationship with God and others, a relationship in which each person makes a gift of his or her self to another and is fulfilled through a generous, committed, and mutual love.[21] This is not to say that every person in a Christian community must be an intimate friend with every other person, but it does mean our churches should be communities in which people respect one another, support one another, challenge one another, encourage one another, love one another, and share together a gracious and hopeful vision of life. In such communities real friendship can be learned and blessed intimacy experienced.

This is not to idealize our churches; rather, it is to challenge them to be what they are called to be. The church is not primarily a place where we go, but a people we promise to be. The church is the community where people through baptism are initiated into a way of life that ought to be in deliberate contrast to the system of consumerism and individualism. This initiation remains unfinished; in fact, what baptism begins must continue and be constantly rehearsed in worship. The liturgy and worship of the church, as we suggested in chapter 1, should form us in the very values, attitudes, dispositions, and practices that not only teach us about intimacy and friendship but help us become capable of achieving them. More emphatically, as a *sacrament of initiation,* the aim of baptism and our subsequent worship is not to produce a "good consumer" but a good person, a saint, a true friend of God who knows what it means to be a true friend of others.[22]

Why so? Because in worship we discover there is no need to hide who we are, much less any need to market or sell ourselves. The God who knows us infinitely better than we know ourselves—indeed, knows everything about us—loves us and accepts us. To worship God is to be "found out" by God. Through worship we are freed to know ourselves as we truly are, sinful and broken and incomplete but nonetheless perfectly loved. Worship responds to the deep human need to be found out by another, the deep human need to be seen and known for exactly who we are, *and still be loved.* We long for someone to know us inside and out, and God does. We long for someone to know all there is about us, the shameful as well as the flattering, and still love us, and God does. This dynamic of being found out and accepted should happen to all of us when we enter into the merciful and saving narratives of God.

One of the delusions promoted by our culture is that intimacy is instant and easily achieved, but if our analysis is correct, it suggests there are barriers and impediments to intimacy in all of us. The kind of healing, purification, and interior transformation necessary for intimacy and friendship takes time; it requires not only that we be patient and hopeful with ourselves but that others are as well. The church should be this kind of community not only for one another but in their dealings with everyone. The church should be the befriending community of a befriending God, a God who is patient, hopeful, and faithful with all of us. Whether we struggle with overdetachment, possessiveness, crippling fears, or insecurities, we need to be healed if we are to know and enjoy the grace of true intimacy and friendship. Such healing and gracious restoration should come to us first from God and second from God's faithful community. If our lives have been almost irreparably broken by infidelity, betrayal, and violence, the love we need must first take the form of a healing as we are gradually brought back from death to life, from despair to hope. We should be able to find such a power-

ful, restorative love in God and in the community—the church—
which pledges to embody God's ways.

The Qualities and Characteristics of Friendship

My students, alas, are not always interested in theology, but
one foolproof way to get them talking is to begin a discussion
of friendship. I ask my students to reflect on what they believe
are the essential characteristics of a friendship. The words come
gushing forth: "love," "trust," "a sense of humor," "care and concern," "loyalty," "truthfulness," "affection," "patience," "forgiveness." The students may not always be enjoying such friendships
in their lives, but they know there are qualities that distinguish
friendships from other relationships.

There is no exhaustive list of the qualities of good friendships,
and the priority of these qualities may be slightly different for
all of us, but the following characteristics seem essential to any
real and deep friendship.

First, every friendship begins in some kind of *attraction*. There
is something about another person that catches our attention
and draws us to them. It may be some aspect of their personality or character, such as their goodness or their sense of humor.
It may be their appearance, something as simple as the way they
smile. We may be drawn to them by their overall outlook on life
or by how they treat other people. More often than not, we are
attracted to these potential friends because we sense in them
agreement with what we believe, value, and think important.

The origin of any friendship is rooted in the power of attraction. This makes friendship a selective and preferential love.
We are not friends with everyone because we are drawn to some
people more than to others and to some not at all. We cannot
be friends with people to whom we are in no way attracted or
with whom we sense absolutely no compatibility; nor, obviously, can we be friends with people we find completely revolt-
ing. We have to believe there is something we share in common
with another that is sufficient for us to connect with them in
friendship.

That friendship begins in an attraction to another may be an
obvious point, but it is an important one because it reminds us

we really cannot be friends with just anyone. I cannot have a friendship with a person whose attitudes, values, outlook, and behavior are deeply at odds with my own—for instance, someone who enjoys cruelty or takes pleasure in humiliating others. Sometimes it is realizing a fundamental incompatibility that brings a relationship to an end. We may think we can be friends with someone and even want very much to be friends with them, but as the relationship unfolds we realize there are elements to their character that make connecting with them in a way necessary for friendship impossible.

Second, friends have to like one another. Again, an obvious point but an extremely important one. Sometimes we try to make ourselves friends with people because we think we should be friends with them, but the truth is we really do not like them. Friends are supposed to like doing things together and spending time together, but what happens when we must spend time with people we really don't like? Time passes slowly, sometimes painfully. We feel awkward and uncomfortable in such situations because it is hard for us to be ourselves. Just the opposite happens when we are with people we like and enjoy being with. Time passes quickly, and far from feeling uncomfortable, we can relax and be ourselves with them in ways we cannot with others.

But we must be careful. Basing friendship on attraction and another's likability risks making it unjustifiably exclusive. Friendships are special relationships, but they should not be elitist, and friendships should be characterized by magnanimity, not snobbery. We may not be able to be friends with everyone, but one of the gifts of good friendships should be to teach us how to reach out in kindness and thoughtfulness to others, even those we would rather avoid. True friendships should always make our world bigger, not smaller, by encouraging us to see everyone more compassionately and magnanimously. Friendships are corrupted—indeed, they become morally and spiritually dangerous—when their effect is to leave us ignoring the neighbors Jesus calls us to love. Christian theology has rightly been concerned about the potential pitfalls of friendship precisely because friendship is a preferential and highly selective love. The possible dangers of preferential love must be taken seriously and vigilantly guarded against. It is also true these dangers can be avoided when we remember a healthy friendship is one that teaches us how to be open and receptive to others, even to those whose principal expertise is to drive us crazy.[23]

It is also true that even the best friends do not *always* like one another, simply because none of us is always likable. There are periods in every friendship where we do not like our friends and they probably do not like us. We disappoint one another. We are moody and unresponsive. Some days we are petulant and they are distant. Other days they lash out at us or we seem indifferent to them. This is part of the history of every friendship and why virtues such as patience, forgiveness, and a good sense of humor are indispensable for friendship. Friends come to know one another over time, but sometimes the very qualities we first found endearing in our friends we later find immensely aggravating: the nervous laugh that once seemed so charming now makes us want to scream, or the chattiness we thought was refreshing now makes us wonder if vows of silence are so bad after all.

The longer the friendship, the more we reveal about ourselves. Initially, friends tend to show only their most flattering qualities, but it is impossible to hide our blemishes and flaws forever. There are seasons to every friendship just as there are seasons to any marriage, and good friends work through them because they care for one another and do not want to lose the gift of their friendship, even when sustaining it is hard.

Third, as mentioned above, friends enjoy being together and spending time together. Aristotle said friends who do not spend time together do not remain friends for very long. This isn't necessarily true, but we have to wonder about any "friendship" when friends who used to search for ways to be together now search for reasons to be apart. We might also wonder about "friends" who spend less and less time together and are not bothered by it. One sign of a healthy relationship is that friends delight in one another's company and find themselves uplifted when they are together. We see evidence of this in the best of friendships. These people talk and share and laugh with each other in ways that seldom happen in the other settings of their lives. Being with the friend makes everything more enjoyable, even the most mundane and ordinary tasks of life such as shopping, cooking, studying, cleaning, going to a movie, or eating. Think how dif-

ferent it is to eat alone rather than dine with a friend. Being with
the friend changes the whole meaning of the activity.

By contrast, we wonder about a friendship that increasingly
leaves us feeling morose, gloomy, or depressed. If we walk away
from relationships feeling despondent, burdened, and sometimes diminished, we have to wonder about the relationship and
its overall effect on us. There are always challenges to a friendship, and usually some frustrations and heartache, but overall
a friendship should not have a depressing and dispiriting effect
on us. It is important to stress this because many times we insist
on naming as friendships the very relationships that do us the
most harm or leave us profoundly unhappy. One sign of a good
friendship ought to be joyfulness of spirit, not dejection.

Fourth, friendships should be *freeing relationships*. One of the
great gifts of a good friendship is that each friend helps the other
grow in freedom by helping them be more fully and authentically who they are called to be. Friends have insight into each
other. In fact, sometimes our friends see us better than we see
ourselves. Because they want what is best for us, they use the
knowledge they have of us not only to call us to our best self but
to help us be our best self. They realize we will only know true
freedom when we grow more fully into the grace of our own
identity—the image of God that is uniquely us—and through the
attention and care they extend to us they help with this growth.
Through them we are encouraged to be who God calls us to be.
Their friendship gives us the security we need to courageously
embrace the vocation entrusted to us regardless of what it might
ask of us.

Moreover, to say friendships ought to be freeing relationships
does not deny that in important ways friendships restrict us.
The very nature of a friendship is to forge bonds of loyalty and
commitment between ourselves and others. To be sure, friendships are essentially *obliging relationships* because they create
justified expectations and responsibilities between friends. In
this sense, friendships are inherently limiting. It is precisely
because I am this person's friend that I have obligations to her
I do not have to others, and she has a right to expect certain
things of me a stranger would not. Similarly, friendships may
not always seem freeing when our friends challenge and correct
us, or when they speak the truth we do not want to hear.

Part of the debt we owe our friends is that they help us work through all the things that keep us from being free, whether it be our fears and anxieties, our excessive insecurities or compulsions, elements of our past history and relationships, family situations, character flaws, painful memories, or moments of failure. There is much in each of us that works against the freedom God wants us to have, and one of the great gifts of a friend is not only to give us insight about what those hindrances to freedom and happiness might be but also to help us eventually overcome them.

I learned the importance of this gift of friendship from a student. She wrote an essay on how she had helped a friend find freedom through forgiveness. Her friend's parents had divorced because her father had had an affair with another woman and left his family. The young woman saw what her father's unfaithfulness had done to her mother and siblings, but she also felt keenly the pain and loss it had brought to herself. Understandably, this daughter of divorce was angry and bitter towards her father, but my student worried what that anger and bitterness might be doing to her friend. She feared that her friend was so consumed by her hurt and resentment that it was robbing her of freedom. It was as if she remained captive to her father's abandonment to the point that she would perpetually be victimized by it.

This young woman talked to her friend. She told her she understood her grief and bitterness but worried that this pain of the past was controlling and consuming her. In what I thought took tremendous courage, she told her friend she thought she would have to begin to forgive her father, no matter how difficult it might be, because it was only through forgiveness that she could be freed. She told her that she would do everything she could to help her work through this loss because she knew it was not a burden she could carry alone. I was inspired by this student's deep understanding of both the gift and the responsibilities of friendship and consider it a powerful example of how friends can free us in ways we may not always be able to free ourselves.

We should also note that friendships should be freeing relationships because good friends, as mentioned above, do not try to control or manipulate us, which is a serious abuse of a friendship. Nor do they cling to us in ways that make it difficult for us to have friendships with anyone else. Friendships should cultivate in us a healthy, strong sense of identity and independence. They should encourage us to develop relationships with others or to become involved in activities that may not always include our friends. Doing so is not a threat to the friendship precisely because the friends are confident of the bond of affection, love, and respect between them. One clear difference between an infatuation and a good friendship is that an infatuation always diminishes personal freedom and true friendships augment it.

Fifth, friendships are characterized by *benevolence*, which means friends want what is best for one another and are committed to seeking one another's good. One clear way of determining who our true friends are is simply to reflect on the people we trust to consistently want what is best for us. Not only do our friends desire what is best for us, they also commit themselves to helping us achieve it. Every friendship entails wholehearted devotion to the good of another, and this devotion demands time, energy, creativity, and attentiveness.

This devotion to the other is not seen as a burden to begrudge or an onerous obligation, because what brings us delight and happiness is working for the good of our friends. There are many ways to do this, and one of the skills friends soon develop is being alert to all the various opportunities we have to contribute to the well-being of our friends. Sometimes benevolence is a timely phone call, sometimes it is an invitation to lunch or a movie, often it is little more than making our friend laugh or being there when they need someone to listen. No matter what form this insightful and very personal love takes, seeking the good of the friend is a central activity in the life of any friendship. This indicates why real friendship requires a special kind of person, a person of generous and thoughtful spirit who is capable of looking beyond himself and living for the sake of another.

Nonetheless, even though benevolence is necessary for friendship, it is not enough. In order for there to be a friendship, the benevolence we offer another must be returned to us in kind. Thus, the sixth characteristic of friendship is *mutuality*. We have all had the experience of seeking the good of someone we love but never having our affection and care reciprocated. We reach out to them in friendship, showing our attentiveness through acts of kindness and interest, but the attention we offer them is never offered back to us. This is frustrating and often painful, because in such situations we know the person we wish for a friend does not want us for a friend. The benevolence of friendship must be mutual, but it cannot be coerced. Simply wishing well to another and doing good for her may be a friendly act and an invitation to friendship, but it does not make a friendship, because the good we want for another must be wished for us in return.

Mutuality tells us that friendships cannot be one-sided. Friendships are relationships in which each person is committed to the other and each does good things for the other. Just as one person cannot make a marriage work, friendship demands the investment of two people in each other's well-being. We may love someone very much and give ourselves to seeking his good, but unless our love is returned, it is kindness, not friendship. In a friendship each person knows the good he or she wishes the other is wished for them in return.

The importance of mutuality for friendship suggests that the ideal of love—the most authentically human love—is mutual, reciprocal love. It is important to note this because sometimes in Christianity we have upheld self-sacrifice as the most excellent and exemplary love, the love in light of which all other loves must be evaluated. Obviously, sacrifice is an indispensable ingredient to love, perhaps especially the love of friendship, because all of us are sometimes called to sacrifice for the sake of another. Yet the aim of love is not sacrifice but the mutuality, sharing, and intimacy by which a true union of souls is achieved. In other words, sometimes love only lives when we are able to sacrifice for the sake of another, but the purpose of sacrificial love is to nurture and sustain a relationship. Indeed, even the sacrificial love of Christ crucified was not an end in itself but a revelation of the limitlessness of God's faithfulness and God's unquenchable desire to seek friendship and communion with us.

A seventh characteristic of friendship is that friendships are formed around *shared goods* that help define the purpose and nature of the friendship, as well as the type of friendship. Friendships grow from a whole assortment of interests, cares, and activities we have in common with other people and would hope to pursue with them because we like them and enjoy their company. Friendships can be formed around a common interest in sports, music, movies, gardening, cooking, wine tasting, hobbies, work projects, or church activities, or a shared major in college. But they can also form when people discover they share the same values and convictions and agree on what they consider most important in life. Sometimes people become friends because they share a passion for justice and a desire to help people in need. Sometimes people become friends because they sense in someone deep agreement in religious matters, whether it be the desire to live the values of the Gospels, be more faithful disciples, or grow together in holiness and love. These shared goods, interests, and activities determine the nature and purpose of a friendship and indicate what the life of a friendship will be.

Each of our friendships is different, not only because each of our friends is different but also because the interests, concerns, goods, and activities around which the friendships develop are different. If we want to understand what makes the various friendships of our lives unique, we have to look at the personality, character, and temperament of our friends and the history of our relationship with them. We also need to consider the various goods and activities that identify the friendship and explain the life of the friends. Friendships can be built around most anything, but what those friendships will be and the place they have in our lives will depend on the shared interests that connect us to our friend. This is why, for example, we are not friends with all our friends in the same way or for the same reason. What differentiates the friendships of our lives are the interests, goods, and activities that identify and characterize the friendships. There will be as many different kinds of friendships in our lives as there are interests and activities we share with our friends, and they will vary in intensity, depth, and intimacy according to the nature of the goods we share with them. In general, the more we share in common with a person, the richer and more lasting a friendship will be. The best friendships are not built around a single interest but a variety of interests, goods, and activities the friends enjoy together.

This emphasis on friends sharing something in common helps us understand why we cannot be friends with everybody.

We have to find some way of sharing life with a person for friendship to be possible. We cannot connect in friendship with people with whom we share absolutely nothing in common or with people who are unlike us in every way. Could we be friends with someone who totally despised God or someone who was completely cynical and bitter? Or, perhaps more commonly, with someone who had many good interests but none of them, unfortunately, were ours? Sometimes, for instance, people love one another and consider marrying but discover they do not have enough in common to make the friendship of marriage possible.

Of course, a danger here is to think we must choose as friends only people who are just like us, but nothing would be duller than to select friends who were like us in every respect. One reason we like our friends and want to be with them is precisely because they are *not like us*. They are different in ways that can make the friendship not only interesting but an unfolding adventure. Indeed, it is likely that some of our closest friends are the very people who are unlike us in some very interesting ways, but again, friends cannot be different in every respect. Friendship is a blend of likenesses and differences. There must be enough similarities among friends for them to connect in friendship, but there must also be enough differences for the friends to appreciate each other's uniqueness.

It is by sharing together in the goods and activities of the friendship that friends come to know one another and grow in intimacy and closeness. Spending time with our friends on projects and activities that interest both of us brings us closer to them and deepens the mutuality of the friendship. Whether we are going to a movie or concert together, studying together, or doing volunteer work together, when we are with our friends we learn more about them (and about ourselves) and discover why we enjoy being with them. Most often, however, this deepening mutuality and intimacy occurs from conversations we have with our friends. The more we talk with our friends, the more we reveal about ourselves and the more they disclose about themselves. Spending time with our friends gives us opportunities to share more of who we are with them. As this sharing occurs, the affection we have for our friends deepens and the bond between us grows stronger.

Finally, an eighth quality of friendship is *trust and faithfulness*. Friends have to trust one another and be faithful to one another. Think about how a friendship changes as soon as we wonder whether we can trust a friend. If trust is lacking, we become much more cautious and guarded about what we share with our friends and begin, albeit slowly, to withdraw from the friendship. One of the basic activities of any good friendship is confiding in our friends. We share things with our friends we do not share with anyone else, not only because we want them to know us but also because we trust them. Friends *confide in one another*. They share the secrets, dreams, worries, hopes, and fears of their hearts; they share *confidences*. Confidence literally means to "have faith in one another," and this is essential for any friendship. If friends lose faith in one another, the friendship dies—or becomes very superficial—unless they find a way for trust to be restored.

Think about what you have shared with your friends over the years. Friendship is a gradual unveiling of the self to another. All of us want someone to know us completely. We want another person to know our spirit and soul, but there is a tremendous vulnerability in opening ourselves to another so fully, which is why loyalty, trust, and faithfulness are essential virtues for a friendship and why nothing wounds a friendship more than betrayal and infidelity. Friends talk; in fact, a friendship is like an extended, ongoing conversation, and eventually friends talk about themselves. We test our friendships by deciding what to reveal to our friends. At first we share only what is safe, but eventually we tell them things about ourselves that are not so safe: our deepest fears, the regrets of our lives, our failures, and even the things for which we are ashamed.

Such sharing is crucial to the life of any friendship but is also risky because it puts us in the power of another person. Knowledge, especially intimate knowledge of another, is power. We sometimes speak of this when we say our friends know us "inside and out" or that they know us in ways no one else does. The knowledge we have of our friends is a sacred trust for which we are morally accountable. Put differently, one of the ways our friends honor us is to reveal to us the deepest dimensions of who they are. We honor our friends when we not only respect what they share with us but use that knowledge to help them. We dishonor our friends when we violate the faith and trust they have in us. Friends feel free to be open with us in ways they are not with others because they believe we care for them and want what is best for them; indeed, they entrust themselves to us in the confidence that we will not betray them. It is this great confidence friends have in one another that explains why betrayal in friendship is so wounding and not something from which a friendship quickly recovers.

In this chapter we have probed the mysteries of intimacy by first exploring some of the characteristics of our culture, as well as some of the qualities in ourselves, that can frustrate the development of intimate, abiding friendships in our lives. This reminds us that we cannot take good friendships for granted because friendships require both fitting contexts in which to grow and persons of a certain kind of character. We then examined some of the essential characteristics of friendship in order to recognize what distinguishes friendships from the other relationships of our lives, and also to know why every relationship we call "friendship" may not be worthy of the name. The conviction shaping all of these reflections is that friendship is one of God's greatest gifts to us, a grace for which we remain forever indebted. To see why this might be true is the subject of chapter 3.

three

Why There Are Some Debts We Can Never Repay

The Good Things Good Friends Do for Us

There's an old Latin proverb (all Latin proverbs are old!) that says: "They take the sun from heaven who take friendship from life." We know this is true. Our lives would be terribly impoverished without the gift of our friends. Sometimes we realize the preciousness of friendship only when we experience its fragility: our dearest friend moves to another part of the country or a lifelong friend suddenly dies. At those moments we experience a tremendous sense of loss, perhaps even fear, because it is hard for us to imagine our lives without our friends. What are the good things good friends do for us? In this chapter, I want to reflect on the gift of friendship to our lives and why we owe our friends a debt we can never repay. What do friends do for us that we could not do without them? There are numerous ways to answer this, but I want to focus on five dimensions of the gift of friendship.

First, perhaps the most fundamental moral value to friendship is that friendships teach us how to care for others. Every friendship is a lesson in the discipline of love because the very nature of a friendship is to teach us to be concerned about something other than ourselves. Friendships draw us out of ourselves and challenges us to be attentive not to our own immediate interests and needs but to the interests and needs of another. In this respect, every friendship entails at least minimal self-transcendence. As we saw before, the distinctive activity of friendship is to be interested in another person for her own sake and to be routinely devoted to her good. None of this is possible if we remain self-centered and self-absorbed.[1]

All of us must be able to learn lessons in caring somewhere, and friendship is a fitting context for doing so. Think of all we can be called to do for our friends, things that call us out of ourselves and challenge us to act on behalf of another. We are called to give time to our friends. We are asked to make sacrifices on their behalf. We are challenged to be patient with them and forgive them. We are expected to stand by them during times of failure or difficulty. We are expected to be loyal to them even when doing so comes with a cost. All of these elements of friendship are morally important because through them we learn how to care deeply for others and to identify closely with them and their good.[2]

But to care for and give ourselves to another person consistently is neither easy nor natural. It is a challenge to be committed to another's good continually. All of us can do this for a while, especially in the early stages of a relationship or when doing good for another is easy, but eventually we feel the "discipline" of love and our zeal falters. This is what makes faithful friendships so ethically praiseworthy. Seeking the good of another steadily and routinely is a high moral achievement, not the least because there are stubborn tendencies in all of us to put ourselves first. One of the gifts of friendship is that it helps us overcome everything in us that prompts us to be selfish and petty and aids us in conquering the things about us that work against our capacity to care for others. In short, friendship teaches us how to love.

In order to love another well we must know them. Friends seek one another's good, but to truly do good for another demands that we first take time to know them *as other*. We spoke earlier of the importance of benevolence for friendship, but benevolence is not an anonymous, undifferentiated regard for the well-being of our friend, as if everyone's good was exactly the same or everyone's needs were identical. All of us are different in important ways, and a skill a good friend must have is the ability to recognize those differences and be attentive to them. We cannot practice benevolence toward our friends without trying to know as best we can their special needs, interests, desires, and concerns, their likes, and their dislikes. The benevolence of friendship must be *personal;* it must be thoughtful and insightful. This is one reason we do not love any two friends in exactly the same way. We love them in light of their differences. We love them because we recognize and esteem their uniquenesses and take their uniquenesses into account in caring for them.

In friendship we learn that in order to love and care for another we must see them as someone other than ourselves. This sounds obvious, but it is notoriously difficult to achieve. So often our love for others is little more than a wily projection of our own needs and desires. Benevolence in friendship means we must break free from the confines of our own perspective in order to discover the needs, cares, and interests of our friend. The only way to do so is to *see the friend as other,* to see her in her uniqueness and to honor it. We know we are loved well in friendship when our friends have taken time to recognize what makes us different from them and what specifically would be best for us.

Second, good friends teach us about ourselves, including aspects of ourselves we might prefer not to know. Friendships are an important source of knowledge and understanding about ourselves, not only because our best friends come to know us better than anyone else but also because sometimes our friends know us better than we know ourselves. It is important to know and understand ourselves, but it is not easy because all of us have only limited knowledge about ourselves, and sometimes the little we do know is tainted by self-deception, insecurity, or a poor self-image. One result of such self-deception and fear is that we are not always the best judges of our character, our dispositions, our needs, and our desires. All of us are experts at rationalization. Often, then, the people closest to us see things about us we may not see at all. For instance, they may encourage us to develop talents we did not know we had or to take chances we would otherwise avoid. Friends give us insight about our identity—who we are essentially as a person—and we need this knowledge to grow and mature.[3]

What makes friendship a source for self-knowledge? Remember how a friendship begins. A friendship starts when two people intuitively sense in one another some similarity of interests and concerns. They sense they hold similar values and principles, perhaps a common understanding of life, and maybe the same dreams and aspirations. They reach out to one another with the invitation of friendship because they believe there is between them an affinity of interests, a compatibility of character, and some kinship of soul that would make good friendship possible.

As the friendship grows, each friend is able to see something of herself in the other because of all they have in common. If another person has values and ideals similar to my own, I can see something of myself in her because I can presume that what is happening to me by pursuing these values must be similar to what I see happening to her. If, for instance, I see my friend becoming more just and more considerate, or more patient and less judgmental of others, I know something of the same transformation may be taking place in me.

No one friend can reflect our whole self back to us, and it would be unfair and unreasonable to expect this. One reason we need a variety of friends in our lives is that no single person can mirror us completely. Each friend brings something special about us to light. Every friend mirrors us, but each does it a different way and to a different degree. One friend may reflect a particular aspect of our character because that is what his friendship elicits from us, but may not mirror other dimensions of ourselves at all. This does not mean he has fallen short as a friend or has been inept at friendship. It simply means every friend is skilled at teaching us something important about ourselves, but no one friend can teach us everything. For instance, with some friends I am reflective, with others I am more playful. With some I may discuss theology, with others Louisville's basketball team or the Green Bay Packers, and with a few I may pray. Each of these is an element of who I am, and each is a tribute to the artistry of a particular friend whose commitment to the same concerns has helped me develop these qualities.

Friendships teach us that through love we make one another "visible" and bring each other more fully to life. It is precisely because no single person can elicit all that is graceful and lovely in another that we need a variety of friends and should not be jealous when our close friends find new friends. Through their own distinctive care and concern, they can draw our attention to some aspect of our friend that we have overlooked. Every person brings something important about our friends out into the open; every person helps mirror some attribute of our friend not only to them but also to us. We should be grateful when our friends find new friends because through them we can discover something new about our friend and see again why we care for her so deeply. The more others reveal the unique goodness of our friends to us, the more we can love them and delight in them.[4]

A third gift of good friendships is that our friends help us stay committed to the most important goals, projects, and aspirations of our lives. We need some way to sustain our zeal and enthusiasm for the projects and purposes to which we have given our lives exactly because it is so easy to become disillusioned with the very ideals that once gave us hope. No matter how worthwhile and attractive a project, activity, or particular way of life might be, inevitably our interest wanes, our commitment weakens, and we begin to doubt its value and question its importance. This is especially true when the cost of keeping a commitment is high.

There is a connection between friendship and fidelity, because friends help us sustain love and appreciation for the most important activities of our lives, especially if they share in them with us. The value of any activity is enhanced when others partake of it as well. Their enthusiasm and devotion reminds us of our own and helps us remember why we made a commitment in the first place. We need other people who care about what we care about, who care about us caring for it, and who care about it *with us*. No matter how worthwhile a project or activity might be, if we are left to pursue it alone it is easy to grow discouraged and indifferent. We begin to wonder if the very absence of others sharing in it with us indicates that it does not have the value and meaning we suspected.

Here too the community of the friends of God, the church, can play an important role. No matter how deep our love for God and our zeal for the gospel might be, a life of discipleship is hard. It may be full of hope, but it is also costly. Eventually every disciple encounters periods of trial and times of discouragement and difficulty. Can anyone truly remain faithful to a life of discipleship if he or she feels alone or suspects that no one else is committed to the same journey? If the church is truly a community of friends committed to a shared life in Christ, then one of the obligations of discipleship is encouraging one another in living that life and helping each other with the tests and challenges of that life. Jesus predicted a cross for all of his followers, but he never said we had to bear those crosses alone. One sign of the vitality of the church is when in each congregation we find a community skilled in helping one another in what each knows to be the most important commitment of their lives. If such friendship is absent in our churches, it should not be surprising if people lose heart and are tempted to abandon their baptisms.

Fourth, one of the most indispensable gifts that come to us from our friends is that through them we learn lessons in goodness and virtue. Through them our character is developed. We said before that we are always better for spending time with good friends and that good friends help us to become our best selves. All of this is crucial for our moral and spiritual development because it suggests we grow in goodness and virtue and holiness in company with others who, like ourselves, want to become good. In his *Nichomachean Ethics*, Aristotle said friendship "is some sort of excellence or virtue, or involves virtue, and it is, moreover, most indispensable for life."[5] Good friendships are indispensable for life, Aristotle says, because we become good by spending time with good people. It is often in the company of our friends that we are reminded of the kind of person we want to become and the ideals and values that are important to us.

It is also in the company of our friends that we learn more about what a good life truly is and what it means to be a good person. Our friends give us wisdom about happiness and excellence. They help us understand better what true goodness is and how we can achieve it. Ask yourself what you have learned from your friends. Think about how they have changed you and made you better. For instance, our friends can teach us not to take ourselves too seriously. They can teach us to be more patient and understanding with the foibles of others. They can help us have courage and persevere when faced with hardships. They can teach us what it means to forgive and be forgiven. They can show us how important it is to be generous and just. They can keep us humble.

These are all crucial dimensions of a well-developed character and of a virtuous person that in some way are the handiwork of our friends. One of the great unpayable debts of friendship is to realize that our friends helped us become better than we ever could be by ourselves. By constantly calling us to—and working for—our best selves, they helped us develop in the most promising ways.

Finally, our friends can free us to live more hopefully and truthfully. There are so many people whose lives are caught in narratives of despair. We have spoken already of some of these narratives: the narrative of consumerism and materialism, the narrative of radical individualism. Narratives of despair are legion, so pervasive that we have come to accept them as our reality. Think about the powerful hold the narrative of violence has on our culture today. This is true for the obvious and sickening violence of drive-by shootings, gang wars, and the now all too common incidents of disgruntled workers returning to shoot their former colleagues. We also see the narrative of violence at work in a culture that so prizes competition and rivalry that it teaches us that the only way we can secure our own identity is by dominating and oppressing somebody else. If this seems extreme, consider the themes of many films today or the most popular shows on television.

How do we break free from these narratives of despair? How can we begin to restructure the world in truthfulness and hope? I think we can start with our friends. In some social and cultural settings, friendships are potentially subversive—acts of genuine protest and resistance—because they dare to break free from what is most corrupting and dehumanizing in a culture in order to begin something new. In cultures ruled by the distorting ideologies of consumerism, individualism, and violence, friendships can offer a much more promising and hopeful way of life.

Many of us began to make important changes in our lives when we found a friend who shared our disenchantment. Instead of feeling isolated by our convictions, we discovered a companion who agreed that there has to be something better, something more fulfilling, something worthier of our devotion. Often it is in conversation with our friends that we discover the uneasiness and dissatisfaction we feel about the sovereign narratives of our culture are not entirely unique. Our friends share our disquiet and, like us, want to live by a different truth. This is why C. S. Lewis said "every real friendship is a sort of secession, even a rebellion," and that all good friendships are a "pocket of potential resistance."[6] The radical power of the best of friendships is that they empower us to break free from the destructive fantasies and ideologies of our culture in order to begin something better.

Authentic friendships can be centers of liberation and new life, even acts of hopeful defiance and rebellion, before much in a culture that is unpromising and enslaving. Friendships give us space to rethink our lives. They offer us a context for reflecting on the habits and patterns of our lives and what they are making of us. They offer us the security we need to risk asking why we really are not happy and to inquire about what might be missing from our lives. Best of all, they invite us to imagine much more promising ways of life and give us the courage we need to embrace them. Such friendships are freeing and full of hope, but they can also be threatening to anyone seduced by the narratives of despair. They can be particularly threatening to people in authority, especially if they are part of institutions that perpetuate these narratives of despair.

In her essay "Feminism and Modern Friendship," Marilyn Friedman says every good friendship has "socially disruptive possibilities."[7] This is the case because friendships enable people to break free from the most unpromising and unhealthy dimensions of a culture, so friendships can be powerful sources of social change. Friedman describes how friendships among women encouraged them to envision something better for themselves than the roles ascribed to them in patriarchal societies, but we can see the same dynamics occurring with other marginalized groups in our society. Gays and lesbians have formed organizations such as Dignity so that they have a community not only where their rights and dignity can be respected but also where they can break free from some of the oppressive stereotypes given them by society. Similarly, persons with physical and mental disabilities have organized so that they might envision "socially disruptive possibilities" for themselves, possibilities that offer them the promise for fuller acceptance into the human community.

But why stop there? Should not the church be a community of "socially disruptive possibilities" as well? Indeed, should not a people called to practice the "socially disruptive possibilities" of Jesus' Sermon on the Mount be adept at imagining and practicing more truthful and hopeful ways of life? If the church is truly living as the friends of God, people should be able to see in the church a community that in its life together embodies an act of resistance against all narratives of despair by proclaiming each day the narrative of hope we call the gospel. Is there anything more socially disruptive than a community committed to living a forgiven and forgiving life in a culture practiced in violence? Is not a community pledged to justice socially disruptive in a society too often complacent before the suffering of all the world's victims? One of the invaluable gifts that come to us from our friends is to free us to imagine more hopeful and truthful ways of life. This should surely be a gift that comes to the world from the church when the friends of God are flourishing together in that socially disruptive possibility that is the reign of God.

Earlier we told the story of the love and friendship shared between two people who never expected to meet but who changed one another's lives forever and helped make one another better: C. S. Lewis and Joy Gresham. It is easy to see ourselves in that story because all of us, hopefully, have had friends who entered our lives, became part of us, and changed us in gracious ways. We know that developing and sustaining such relationships is not easy because of dimensions in ourselves and our world that hinder and sometimes destroy them, but we also know we must work to overcome the obstacles and impediments to friendship because without these relationships our lives are painfully diminished.

Good friendships are great graces, gifts for which we should always be grateful, but they are also important in our life with

God and in a Christian's journey of discipleship. In the next two chapters we shall continue our exploration of friendship by considering in depth its role in the Christian life. We shall look first at how Augustine, the great theologian who has shaped Christian thinking from the fourth century to the present, thought of friendship and its place in the Christian life. In chapter 4 we shall focus on *Spiritual Friendship,* the classic work of Aelred of Rievaulx, a Cistercian monk of the eleventh century. In both instances we shall learn more of what it means for Christians to be the friends of God.

four

Confronting the Riddles of Intimacy

Augustine on Friendship in the Christian Life

As we have seen, we live in a society that is obsessed with relationships and captivated with intimacy, but which seems increasingly inept at understanding either. So many people are longing for close friendships where they will be known, loved, and cherished for who they are but either misunderstand those relationships or never have the opportunity to enjoy them. Intimacy is elusive, and sometimes the harder we try to find it, the more frustrated and bereft we become.

This is a dangerous condition of the soul, and one Christians should never accept because human beings are created *from intimacy* and *for intimacy*. We are living, breathing images of a Trinitarian God whose very life is the fullness and perfection of intimacy. Born from this love, we are called to mirror in our lives together the intimacy, friendship, and community we see perfectly displayed in God. *God is intimacy*. God—Father, Son, and Holy Spirit—is a perfect communion of love. If we who are God's images are to know happiness, peace, and contentment, we must realize that true intimacy both begins in God and ends in God. If we are intimate with God, we will know how to be intimate with one another.

Few knew this better than Augustine. He of the famous "restless heart" learned from the many wrong turns of his life that the answer to his heart's longings was to be found not in wealth, not in pleasures, and not even in knowledge, but in a deep, abiding intimacy with God. Augustine also discovered that we cannot separate intimacy with God from intimacy with others, because an incarnational God—a God who took flesh and walked the earth with us in Jesus—works through the love, goodness, and care of others to let us know we are loved and cared for by him. For Augustine, becoming intimate in love with God did not mean turning away from others but turning toward them with a new understanding of what love, friendship, and intimacy mean and why they are so important for the Christian life.

Augustine's insights can help us probe the labyrinth of intimacy today and shed light on some of our confusion. Although it may sound farfetched, if we understand Augustine on friendship, we will see why there should be no loneliness in the church.

Friendship and the Christian Life: A Theological Analysis

What, then, does Augustine say? First, perhaps the most intriguing aspect of Augustine's account of friendship is his claim that we do not choose our friends; they are brought to us by God. For Augustine, our friends, especially our closest and lifelong friends, are God's gifts to us given for providential purposes.[1] Augustine was convinced of Paul's comment in his first letter to the Christian community at Corinth, where Paul asks, "For what do you have which you did not receive?" (1 Cor. 4:7).[2] Like Paul, Augustine came to see everything good as a gift, especially the dearest friends of our lives. We do not instigate these friendships; God does. They are gifts of God's grace, workings of God's providential, infinitely creative, and sometimes very surprising love in our lives. Through all the wrong turns and often painful misdirections of his life, Augustine came to see that intimacy is not something we chase after; it is a grace we unwrap.

Friendships are concrete, highly personal expressions of how God loves us insightfully and redemptively in the actual circumstances of our everyday lives. They are blessed manifestations of how God, like all skilled lovers, knows what is best for us and works, with much grace and creativity, to bring timely gifts into our lives. If benevolence is an attribute of all true friendships, the friends God gives us are examples of God's benevolence actively at work for us. If a friend is someone who seeks our true good and devotes himself to our happiness, then the best friends of our lives are examples of the very practical, ingenious, and care-filled ways God befriends each of us. Sometimes we wonder if God's love is real. Or even if we believe in the reality of God's love, we wonder if *God loves us*. How can we ever be sure? Augustine answers that we know God's love for us is real through the real friends who love us. They do not enter our lives accidentally, but providentially.

This is an interesting way to look at the best and most promising relationships of our lives. Sometimes we meet people we feel we were destined to meet, people who, in the language of Christian theology, must be workings of God's providence because there is no other way we can explain how our lives so unexpectedly collided with theirs. People often talk this way when you ask them to explain the origins of their friendship. The encounter that led to them becoming friends seems like a matter of sheer chance, a startling coincidence that makes them realize how easy it would have been for them never to have met. A difference of a minute would have meant a different chapter in the unfolding story of their lives. But they did meet and, in retrospect, wonder if what they took to be sheer coincidence was actually another example of how God is a clever lover, constantly surprising us with new expressions of that love.

Doesn't this tell us something important about a Christian understanding of intimacy? It tells us that true intimacy both begins in and must always be rooted in God's love. It tells us that any attempt to achieve intimacy apart from God is counterfeit. It says that any intimacy we achieve with another is always preceded by God's intimate love for us, a love that works through grace and the sometimes subtle ways we encounter grace in our daily lives. It suggests that if intimacy is rooted in the creative workings of grace, intimacy is always *life in God through life with another* and will not be found or experienced apart from God or apart from the special relationships of our lives. For Augustine, intimacy always involves a partnership of three: ourselves, others, and the God whose love joins us together and in whose love we must remain. This is why any path to intimacy that sidesteps God is a dead end.

Nonetheless, saying that friendships are gifts of God does not rule out some kind of choice and confirmation on our part. Friendships certainly demand our active response and ongoing cooperation. Grace and choice are not incompatible, because we must act on the graces that come our way; gifts that are freely given must be freely received. Friendship can be both a grace and a decision, both a gift and a choice, because we cannot only refuse the gift, we can also misuse or neglect it. We can say no to the gift, we can take it for granted, we can be careless and unappreciative, or we can receive it gratefully and wholeheartedly, rejoicing in the gift God has entrusted to us and expressing our gratitude by never taking the gift for granted. Friends may be a gift from God to us, but we must act on that grace, live in that grace, and care for that grace. That is one of the reasons true intimacy is hard work, a grace to be nurtured, never neglected, and why there is no deep intimacy without fidelity.

The second quality Augustine sees in Christian friendship is that these relationships that begin in God must be modeled on God and seek God. Christian friendships must be modeled on the inner life of the God we call Trinity, because the triune God is the exemplar of all genuine friendship and all true intimacy. Obviously, Augustine understands this analogously—none of us can love with the perfection and fullness of God. But we can model our love on God's love; we can seek to imitate and grow in God's love. When we do so, we not only participate in the friendship life of God but are also transformed according to it and ultimately become one with it.

What practically would this mean? If we are to imitate God's love, how does the Trinity reveal God as loving? The Trinity tells us that God is not just love but, more precisely, that the very life of God is friendship love. The Trinity reveals God as a community of friendship, a *communion of intimacy* in which love is perfectly given and perfectly received. God is not three disjointed persons, but a communion of persons in which each one bestows life and identity on the others, and each flourishes through the love of the others. The Trinity reveals that the very life of God is a life of *intimate relationship*. No person in the Trinity can exist apart from the others because within the God we worship are three distinct persons intimately and indissolubly connected to one another in love. The Trinity tells us that at the very heart of God we find not solitude or loneliness but intimate, life-giving love. The Trinity reveals God as *shared life*, a community of persons who are absolutely one together and yet perfectly unique in each of its persons.

In the divine friendship, the perfect outpouring of love between Father, Son, and Spirit results in unbroken oneness and a community that is never diminished by rivalry, jealousy, or selfishness. In God we see a community in which persons are not set over against each other, but a community in which friends flourish through freely given love. In God we do not find a community fractured through struggle, conflict, and domination; rather, we see a community in which differences of persons are celebrated, respected, and affirmed.

There is no brokenness in God, no estrangement or alienation. There is nothing in God needing healing, nothing in God requiring reconciliation, because God is the perfection of the intimacy in which each person receives identity, joy, and happiness through the unblemished love of another. There are no breakdowns of love in God. Here God is strikingly different from us. Breakdowns in human love abound. Our love breaks down when resentments build, when jealousies thrive, when pettiness wins the day, and when hurts build up but are not forgiven. Our love breaks down and community dies when people withdraw into themselves, when they stop giving to others, or when they become experts at exclusion rather than embrace. Intimacy is lost for us when mistrust, hostility, and betrayal proliferate, and when we abandon loves we do not have the patience to heal. Intimacy is never lost in God because God's love never fails, God's love never breaks down.

This is how we are to love one another in Christian friendships. For Christians, friendships are never just special relationships; rather, they are *practices of perfection* and *sanctifying ways of life*. Through them we model our lives together on the life and love we see in God. We learn that, like God, all of us find life through love. We learn that love and life go together because the very possibility of having life and of developing and fulfilling our natures as human beings depends on learning how to love and on being loved. The Trinitarian friendship of God teaches us that we are brought to life through love and we live through love. This is true from the beginning of our lives until their end. The inescapable truth shown us by God is that we either love or we perish. Either we learn the grace of intimacy and the secret of community or our lives are haunted by emptiness and loneliness.

If we are God's image and likeness, the love that will draw us to life and perfect us must be similar to the love we see in God. If God is a communion of persons joined together by generous, life-giving, mutual love, then we will grow and flourish only insofar as we practice such love in our own lives. If we imitate the friendship love of God, we will affirm the dignity and identity of one another. We will draw each other more fully to life and, through the love we share, shall become one—not despite our differences but in them. If we imitate the love we see in God, we will love one another in a way that affirms and celebrates our individuality and differences and remember that such love should lead not to division and separation but to unity and peace.

Here too we learn the secret of intimacy. We never find intimacy if we aim for it directly. Quite the contrary, intimacy is the work and achievement of a special kind of love. One of the reasons many people are frustrated in their quest for intimacy is that they forget that sacrifice and other-centeredness are prerequisites of intimacy. Intimacy is the harvest of genuine mutuality, but mutuality is the work of an other-centered and sometimes even sacrificial love. It is when we find joy in living for another, in seeking their good and being devoted to their wellbeing, that we experience intimacy. It is when, like God, we allow our love to bring another to life and delight in affirming their dignity that we forge bonds of unity that may be tested but are seldom broken.

A perfect example of this is Madeline L'Engle's *Two-Part Invention*, which tells the story of her marriage of more than forty years to Hugh Franklin. It is a beautiful chronicle of intimacy achieved, but what Madeline L'Engle learned in her marriage to Hugh is that intimacy grows not so much through the

"romance periods" of a marriage (though they are important)
but through the "give-and-take" of love. At one point she reflects,
"As the years have moved on, our explosions have become far
less frequent as we have learned to live with each other, accepting each other's edges and corners."[3] Accepting each other's
"edges and corners" perfectly expresses both the sacrificial element at the heart of any love capable of intimacy and what it
essentially means to respect "the other." As L'Engle later writes,
"The growth of love is not a straight line, but a series of hills and
valleys."[4] Isn't it often true, whether we are talking about marriage, friendships, or our life together in communities, that the
deepest and most resilient intimacy comes when we are willing
to work through the "hills and valleys" of love by being patient
with one another, being attentive to the needs of the other, and,
when necessary, giving way to the other? Don't we sometimes feel
a deeper unity results when we find in ourselves the humility and
graciousness necessary to accept "the edges and corners" of the
ones we love? This is not to say sacrifice and other-centeredness
are the essence of intimacy, but it is to suggest there can be no
truly satisfying and lasting intimacy without them.[5]

A third characteristic of Augustine's understanding of friendship and its role in the Christian life is that friends are *to live the
life of grace.* As Marie Aquinas McNamara notes in her *Friendship in Saint Augustine,* unlike Cicero or Aristotle (who said for
friends to show benevolence for one another was for them to
wish for each other the highest possibilities of natural virtue and
happiness in this life), Augustine saw Christian friendship envi-
sioning a much different possibility. In Christian friendships,
he believed, each friend wishes for the other a life of holiness
and grace on this earth and everlasting happiness with God and
the saints in heaven.[6] Of course, the good that friends seek for
one another would also include well-being and happiness in this
world, but the primary aim of benevolence in Christian friendships, Augustine believed, was to help one's friends grow in the
new life of grace. To seek what is best for one's friends was not
only to help them make their way in the world but also to help
them make their way to the reign of God and the communion
of saints. The friends would not want one another to lose sight
of the greatest hope and possibility of their lives. Augustine's
friends sought happiness and well-being for one another in a

life of holiness on earth and beatitude in heaven. It is friendship informed by a different narrative vision, a vision that presents, ultimately, a very different understanding of both the purpose and the perfection of the friendship. In the Christian narrative, friendships give us companionship on earth, but their ultimate purpose is to help us gain companionship with God, the angels, and the saints in heaven.

Christian friendship envisions the reign of God. That is its goal and ultimately its most perfect expression, but it envisions the reign of God by striving to live according to it now. Through friends sharing the life of grace, each helps make the other fit for the community of perfect friendship that is the kingdom of God. Aristotle's friendships were "perfecting" by making the friends fit citizens for Athens; Augustine's friends remember that our ultimate citizenship is not in Athens or Rome or any other earthly city, but in heaven, the city of God. The life of grace that comes to us in Christ is a new way of life and a new way of being, and the cumulative effect of pursuing such a life together with our friends should be to make us fit citizens of the kingdom of God by learning and living the love of God. We love our friends best, Augustine knew, when we wish them to love God more than anything and help them to do this. As he wrote in a letter to a friend, " . . . we truly love our neighbours as ourselves if, as far as we are able, we lead them to a similar love of God."[7]

In such friendships, the friends, joined together in Christ, not only teach one another what it means to love God but also what it means to love *like God*. For Augustine, friendships should help us grow in the love of God, in the sense that through them we love God more deeply and our love becomes more godly. If our friendships with others are patterned on the friendship of God that comes to us in Christ, then through those friendships we are formed or, better, *transformed,* in the love of God, so that eventually the way we love our friends resembles the way God loves us. This is what should happen through the life of friendship. We should (1) teach each other about the love of God, (2) form each other in the love of God, and (3) help each other practice the love of God. For Augustine, such friendships are "schools of love" and perfecting ways of life.[8]

This gives a different slant to how we understand intimacy. In the Christian narrative, intimacy has a *theological character.*

The purpose of intimacy is more than to offer us kinship and consolation in our everyday life. In the Christian narrative, the purpose of intimacy is to deepen our life together in God so that together we can enjoy the fullness of friendship with God in communion with all the saints. What Augustine hints through his analysis of friendship and its role in the Christian life is that the aim of intimacy is to help us grow in the love of God and to live our lives together in God by pursuing the new way of being— the life of grace that comes to us in Christ. We only experience intimacy when we are *in God* and *living for God*. The deeper our life in God, the deeper our intimacy with one another. This is why, to put it bluntly, for Christians, intimacy begins not with sex but with prayer.

Linking intimacy with one another to intimacy with God was important for Augustine because it assured him that love for God is not something entirely different from love for one's friends, but that they are indeed connected. Augustine did not want a strong love for friends to compete with or detract from our love for God, which would be the case, for example, with infatuation or any other disordered love. He did not want to see love for God and love for our friends as rival intimacies, but as deeply complementary. He was able to reconcile wholehearted love for God with the command to love our neighbor through his understanding of friendship. In other words, for Augustine, it is not that we love our friends and then love God, but that we love God as we love our friends. In friendship, love of God and love of neighbor come together.

Obviously, Augustine believed that since God is the *summum bonum,* the highest and most perfect good, we should love God more than we love anything else, and we should love everything else in God and in relation to God. Since God is the source of all goodness, indeed, the source of all that we love, all our loves should be directed to God. That is precisely the point. If we direct all our loves to God, including our love for our friends, then friendship does not compete with our love for God, but expresses and deepens it. Augustine did not want our wholehearted love for God to require a halfhearted love for our friends. And he was able to avoid this unhappy conclusion by suggesting that since God comes to us in our friends and we love God with and through our friends, love for our friends does not rival or conflict with our love for God, but is one with it.

In this way, Augustine was able to avoid two things. First, by saying we are to love God in our friends and to love our friends in God, he could avoid the problem of "loving the creature more than the Creator,"[9] something Augustine, after his conversion, sometimes feared about good, passionate friendships. A reasonable fear about the strong and enduring friendships of our lives is that they could draw us away from God. Sometimes this happens when friends become overly focused on themselves or when they foster attachments or develop pastimes that can make them unmindful of God and oblivious to the true purpose of their lives. Such dangers can be avoided, Augustine knew, if we see love for God and love for our friends not in opposition, which would have required the rejection of friendship in the Christian life, but so intimately connected that each love complements and serves the other. This is why one sign of genuine intimacy is that it makes us more centered in God and more mindful of God, not less. If this does not happen, the intimacy is counterfeit and morally and spiritually dangerous.

Second, by uniting love for God with friendship, loving God wholeheartedly does not have to come at the expense of loving our friends. Wholehearted attentiveness and devotion to God does not require inattentiveness and neglect of our friends. Quite the contrary, by uniting love of God with love for our friends, Augustine gave the highest possible value to the human love called friendship. Friendship is not a lesser love or a defective love—a love for which Christians must apologize—but a supremely excellent love that is indispensable for the Christian life. Friendship is the most fitting way for us to encounter God, come to know God, love God, and grow together toward God. Indeed, friendship becomes a kind of sacrament, a vital sign of God's active and personal love for us and our active and very personal love for God.

A fourth characteristic of Augustine's understanding of friendship is that the shared life of friendship, sustained over time, brings such a rich, deep intimacy and unity to the friends that the friends become one in spirit and soul. Like many of his contemporaries, Augustine was greatly influenced by Cicero's treatise on friendship. He was intrigued by Cicero's comment that because of all friends share in common and the time they spend together, they grow increasingly closer to one another in a deep unity of heart and soul.

Augustine experienced this gift of friendship in his own life. He knew an intimacy and unity among friends that was so deep and abiding that it was as if from two or more distinct and separate persons a communion of persons emerged. This fascinated Augustine. He was passionately attracted to the idea that love creates unity by overcoming all that divides us. He often remarked, when discussing friendship, that through friendship many become as one (*ex pluribus unum facere*).[10] The bond of friendship creates oneness among the friends, a unity that makes them feel they are one in heart, in soul, and in mind. In a letter to Jerome in which he discusses his friendship with Alypius, Augustine wrote, "Anyone who knew us both would say that we were two separate people only as to our bodies, not our minds, for we are in complete agreement and on terms of perfect intimacy although we differ in merit in which he surpasses me."[11] Through the love of friendship, divisions and distances melt away as the friends, through all that is shared between them, achieve a true and lasting communion of persons.

Augustine's conviction about the intimacy and unity possible in friendship intensified after his conversion. He believed an even greater intimacy was possible for Christians because they were joined to one another in Christ. Baptism united them to Christ and thus to one another, and the more they lived their lives in Christ and loved one another in Christ, the more they became one in heart, mind, spirit, affection, and soul. For Augustine, the greatest possible intimacy and unity among human beings is intimacy and unity in Christ, and this unity is the foundation for peace. Again, shouldn't Augustine's account of the intimacy possible for friendships founded in Christ be a fitting description for the church today? Shouldn't our churches be communities where people see and experience a unity among persons that does not deny their differences or erase their distinctiveness, but works to overcome all that divides them? If Augustine is correct, the church should be a "community of peace" not because everyone always agrees with everyone else, but because in Christ and in the life they share together they know an intimacy and unity much deeper and far more resilient than whatever can possibly divide them.

Augustine desperately wanted to believe unity was possible among people and that people could live together in peace. He also wanted to believe this because he saw so little unity and peace in his world. As Peter Brown illustrates in his magisterial biography of Augustine, Augustine lived during a time characterized not by unity and peace but by disharmony and conflict both in society and in the church.[12] Unity and peace were shattered inside the church by schism and heresy, and they were shattered outside the church by wars and insurrection. With so much dissension, bitterness, chaos, violence, and bloodshed surrounding him, it was imperative for Augustine to find a way human beings could overcome the dark forces of division and conflict in order to live together in community and peace. He found his answer in friendships and communities where people were united together in Christ, the one who came to overcome all that estranges us from one another and to show us how to be one.

All this talk of wars and insurrection may seem irrelevant for our understanding of intimacy today, but in a world that is so often structured and habituated in practices that undermine intimacy, it surely isn't. Intimacy breaks down through the "wars and insurrections" in our own lives. It breaks down, whether in our world, our churches, or our lives, when bitterness and dissension flourish. Intimacy is lost when barriers come between us and, instead of working to budge them, we allow them to harden. Intimacy weakens when conflicts divide us, when suspicions proliferate, when gossip becomes the language of community, when lying becomes routine, and when prevailing becomes more important than repenting. Can intimacy be sustained apart from the peace of Christ? Can we ever be one if we have not first learned from Christ that unity is the work of forgiveness, that there is no intimacy without patience, and that there can be no oneness among persons without truthfulness? Intimacy is a measure of the love that lives between us, and Augustine knew there is no more resilient, hopeful, faithful, and skilled love than the love we are baptized into, and pledge to learn, when we are immersed into the life, death, and resurrection of Christ.

But unity is not always a mark of the church. We have all heard of or, sadly, been part of faith communities that were torn apart by theological differences that had hardened into ideologies. Our churches are fractured by groups that are each convinced its own way is not only the right way but the only way and by people whose bitterness, hostility, and maliciousness drive many away and defeat the spirits of those who remain. One of the most glaring scandals in our churches today is that people do not find community among persons there, much less the peace of Christ. Instead, they too often find a malaise that suggests pettiness and self-righteousness have conquered. Such congregations may be quite articulate at describing the love of Christ and the importance of salvation, but the emptiness any visitor feels in these places convinces them to search for life elsewhere. More often than not, these congregations, baffled by declining membership, look not to themselves for an explanation of their demise, but blame the "unbelief" of an increasingly secular world.

Augustine had great hopes that Christians could achieve in their lives together an intimacy, unity, and peace every human being longs for but does not always know how to achieve. He believed the most perfect expression of the intimacy and unity that is possible in Christ was the monastic life. Augustine said this not to disparage other forms of life, but he believed that ideally the monastic life gathered people who collectively aspired to seek the highest good possible for human beings in this world: a life that sought to love, praise, and glorify God through love, prayer, friendship, and service with one another. For Augustine, the monastic life not only should be a foretaste of the perfect community of the friends of God in heaven but should also achieve on earth the greatest possible unity and peace among human beings. At the beginning of the rule he wrote for his community, Augustine said, "For you are all gathered together into one body so that you may live in a spirit of unanimity and may have one soul and one heart."[13]

Isn't this a fitting description for the church? Must Augustine's insights be limited to monastic communities? Obviously, monastic communities offer a context and rule of life for achieving unity and peace that may not seem as readily available to others outside them, but Augustine's reflections are relevant for

Christians no matter where we live. The church should be a community where people gather to love, praise, and glorify God through love, friendship, and service to one another. Each congregation should be a community where people strive "to live in a spirit of unanimity" so they "may have one soul and one heart" among them. Augustine's conviction has to be ours: If there is to be any true and lasting peace in the world, it can only come from the peace of Christ. That peace has to be palpable, it has to be visible and believable, and it is the role of the church to make it so.

A fifth characteristic of friendship for Augustine that is illuminating for our understanding of intimacy is that he did not believe physical proximity was necessary for intimacy any more than it was a guarantee for intimacy. Augustine obviously preferred to be together with his friends, but the union he felt with them did not depend upon their living together or even being geographically near one another. Here he was markedly different from Aristotle, who asserted that if friends did not spend significant time together, the friendship could not survive. Augustine felt friends could be hundreds of miles away and seldom see one another but still have intimacy. By contrast, people could spend considerable time together and, in fact, live together for years and never know intimacy. We know this to be true. We can live with people and feel absolutely no connection with them. We can share life with them for years and never get to know them, much less have with them the unity characteristic of good friends. On the other hand, we can be oceans apart from people and know they live in our hearts because of the love and affection that bonds us to them.

Intimacy in friendship hopes for, but does not depend on, physical proximity between friends. Instead, it depends on the goods that join friends together and the purpose that explains their friendship. This was important for Augustine because so many of his friends lived at a distance. He kept in touch with them through letter writing, but it was not the same as being with them. If geographical separation from friends is unavoidable, how can we be sure it will not weaken the friendship? We must do what we can to keep the friendship alive, but it is also true, Augustine knew, that even if friends seldom have opportunity to spend time together, they can still be united in heart and soul because the intimacy of Christian friendship comes not from physical proximity, but through a common vision of faith and shared life in Christ.

The bond of Christian friendship is the bond of grace, the kinship we have with one another in Christ. This is why neither absence nor distance need weaken or destroy a friendship. No matter how far apart friends might be geographically, they are always one *baptismally and eucharistically*. Any person united to Christ through baptism is simultaneously joined to every other person baptized into Christ, and any person who eats the body and drinks the blood of Christ is one with every other person, no matter where they are, who partakes of that feast.

This is expressed beautifully in a letter Augustine wrote to his friend, the future Pope Sixtus, in which he alludes to the famous passage of Romans 5:5 (". . . the love of God has been poured out in our hearts through the Holy Spirit who has been given to us"). Augustine hints that it is this love that unites us together in an intimacy no distance can destroy. He says to his friend, "Whether absent or present in body, we wish to have you in the one spirit by means of which love is poured forth in our hearts, so that wherever we may be in the flesh, our souls will be inseparable in every way."[14]

Moreover, Augustine argued that if the bond of friendship is shared life in Christ, then friends, even when separated, will have much greater intimacy and unity between them than they would if they lived together but were united over a lesser good. For Augustine, the greatest possible intimacy comes not from physical closeness or even physical expression, but from belonging to the body of Christ. This means intimacy is less a matter of sexual expression and more an *ecclesial practice*. It depends more on baptism than sexual technique. This is not to be crass, but it is crucial to underscore the importance of Augustine's insight for us who live in a culture where intimacy is too often and too easily identified with sexual expression. In no way do I want to deny the importance of our bodies for achieving intimacy, but I do want to argue that they are hardly a guarantee for intimacy, as anyone who has experienced the loneliness of promiscuity can attest.

If Augustine were alive today, would he say we need a church in order to experience intimacy? Given his belief that the most authentic, satisfying, and lasting intimacy comes from the union we have with one another in Christ, it would seem the church—the intimate friends of God—should be the community we need to learn and experience an intimacy that does not deceive. A passage from a letter of Augustine captures this powerfully:

> It is not your absence which saddens me, for we are part of that Church which, however far it extends throughout the world, through God's favour forms the one great body of the great head which is the Saviour. As a result, however far apart we are even in the furthest corners of the world, yet we are together in Him in the unity of whose body we remain. How much closer together we are when we are in the same body than we would be even if we lived in the same house![15]

Finally, a sixth characteristic of Augustine's understanding of friendships in Christ is their *eschatological dimension*, which means the friendship, love, intimacy, and unity we enjoy on earth will be perfected in heaven. As Carolinne White observes, "Augustine believed only in heaven can human relationships be perfect, when God will truly be all in all."[16] No wonder intimacy is elusive. No wonder however close we may draw to another human being in love, we are sometimes still haunted by longing and incompleteness. Augustine knew that even the best friendships fall short of satisfying us completely, because the God who is the source and center of any true intimacy is also its completion. The perfect community of friendship, and, therefore, the most perfect and enduring intimacy, is found not on earth but in heaven. Ultimately, the only lasting and perfectly satisfying intimacy is found not in an earthly fellowship but in the city of God, that communion of the blessed that Augustine understood to be a "perfectly harmonious fellowship" where all the saints love one another and together love and enjoy God.[17]

It is in that community of perfect love and perfect mutuality that men and women will "be able to know one another completely and to form a perfect intimacy, as friends aimed to do."[18] The very things to which friends aspire to here on earth but never totally achieve will be perfectly fulfilled in the kingdom of God. There we will know one another through and through, there we will enjoy perfect intimacy and unity, and there we shall know an unshakable peace because, Augustine reasoned, in heaven nothing will threaten or limit our friendship.

Still, no matter how hard we try to know our friends and love them, our earthly relationships always reflect the limitations of our nature, including our sinfulness. Human beings are finite, limited creatures whose deepest longings are hindered by our inescapable contingency. We have all had moments in which the most profound feelings of intimacy can be shadowed by a disturbing and inexplicable loneliness (if only in the awareness that those feelings will not last). Or we can remember situations where the joy we felt in being one with people we love was haunted by an underlying sadness whose origins we could not understand. Such is the destiny of even the best loves, short of the kingdom of God. We strive for a love and unity that can be rich and true but can never completely quench the yearnings of our hearts.

It will be different in the kingdom of God. One of the things that frustrated Augustine about earthly friendships is that no matter how much we may love our friends and want to know everything about them, our knowledge of them and their knowledge of us is always partial, clouded, and incomplete. Love brings knowledge, but only perfect love brings perfect knowledge. This is why we can never completely know our friends' hearts no matter how much we may love them, and why we are never as one with them as we might like. On earth, the barriers to intimacy, despite our best efforts, remain. We can lessen them. We obviously must work to overcome them, but we never escape them completely. This is why the occasional frustration we feel with even the best relationships usually reflects nothing more than the inherent limitations of human possibility, not that the relationship is in trouble, much less that it is time to abandon it.

The eschatological character of Christian friendship gave Augustine great hope because it assured him that the multiple limitations and imperfections of even the best of friendships will be transcended in the kingdom of God. In heaven, friends will enjoy complete knowledge and understanding of one another. In heaven, love will know no more barriers, no more fears. This is why, after his conversion, even though Augustine would grieve the death of a friend, he strongly believed that in death "we do not lose them but send them ahead to the place for which we ourselves are heading; there our love for them will be stronger and our understanding of them deeper, for nothing will remain hidden from our closest friends in that place where everyone is our most intimate friend."[19]

Thus, the kingdom of God is the perfect friendship community where all are joined in love for one another and in love and praise of God. There is continuity between our earthly friendships and our heavenly ones because, for Augustine, the most perfect expression of friendship on earth is one in which the friends' attention is directed to God. In true friendship their hearts are centered on God, and everything they do offers praise and glory to God, something the saints, the real friends of God, do best. Thus, our earthly friendships anticipate and already share in, however incompletely, the perfect friendships of the city of God. For all of their unavoidable limitations, these friendships are indispensable in the Christian life because they prepare us to share in the everlasting fellowship of the friends of God in heaven. As Carolinne White explains, for Augustine, "not only does the Christian have the hope of perfect relationship in the life to come but he can even regard the formation of friendships in this life, imperfect and uncertain though they be, as a foreshadowing of the true unity and intimacy to come, . . . in so far as they are spiritual relationships . . . founded on a shared love of God."[20]

Friendships begun in grace and modeled on the trinitarian love of God never end. What grace begins, beatitude completes in that community of perfect intimacy and lasting peace—the kingdom of God—where there is no enmity, no dissension, and no sadness, and where nobody is lonely because all are one in the love of God. For Augustine, the perfection of friendship is a heavenly liturgy of glory and praise in which each person is joined to every other person and all are joined in love to God.

How the Riddles of Intimacy Are Answered

Intimacy on earth may be elusive, but it is achievable. Created for intimacy, our restless, searching hearts will not know peace until we learn what real intimacy is and what kind of life makes it possible. In a society where so many are lonely and so many paths to intimacy are counterfeit, does the church have something to offer? Is intimacy not so much an individual achievement but both a grace and an ecclesial practice? Should Christians know better than most that the search for intimacy is always also a search for God?

Augustine would answer yes to each of these questions. He knew intimacy is inseparable from God, because God is intimacy, a communion of perfect, life-giving love, the fullness of which is happiness and peace. Our search for intimacy has to take us to God because God is the answer to the great hungers and longings of our hearts. Augustine also knew life with God can only be found through life with one another. The riddles of intimacy are answered not only when our hearts are centered on God but also when they are open to and shared with others. Augustine hardly grasped this the first thirty-three years of his life, but after his conversion this wisdom guided his life. It is a wisdom Aelred of Rievaulx, a twelfth-century monk, knew well and wanted to share with his brothers in community. He did so in *Spiritual Friendship*, a treatise we shall explore in the next chapter.

five

What Medieval Monks Can Do for Us
Aelred of Rievaulx and the Life of Spiritual Friendship

Aelred of Rievaulx was born in Hexham, Northumbria (between England and Scotland) in 1110.[1] The son of a married Catholic priest, as a young man Aelred was a member of the court of King David of Scotland. He entered the Cistercian monastery at Rievaulx in northeastern England in 1134 and was abbot there from 1147 until his death twenty years later.

Aelred began writing *Spiritual Friendship* around 1147/48, but he never envisioned it having a life beyond the monastic walls of Rievaulx, much less being read by us today. His aim was to show his fellow monks at Rievaulx what good friendships should be in the monastic life and how they could aid one's life in Christ. His interest in *Spiritual Friendship* was not to explore friendship in general but to reflect on how friendships could help the monks grow together in their common vocation. Like Augustine, he believed good, healthy relationships should serve one's life in Christ, not hinder it.

More practically, as abbot of the community, Aelred could see relationships forming among his brother monks. Some were healthy and conducive for a life of holiness, but others were not.

97

Some clearly were friendships centered in Christ, but others were puerile infatuations, emotionally intense but spiritually deadening relationships that were detrimental to a monk's life in Christ. What sorts of relationships should he encourage his brothers in community to develop, relationships that could assist them in their religious life? How could friendships support their life in Christ, not draw them away from it? By contrast, what are relationships the monks should avoid? What relationships does Aelred see around him at Rievaulx that may wear the name of friendship, but falsely? These are the questions Aelred asks when he writes *Spiritual Friendship*.

Aelred was influenced by Augustine's account in the *Confessions* of the role of friendships in his life. He was particularly shaped by Cicero's *De Amicitia* (*On Friendship*) and acknowledges his debt to the philosopher in the prologue to *Spiritual Friendship* when he recalls the first time he read Cicero's treatise and the lasting effect it has had on him. Like Cicero's *De Amicitia,* Aelred writes *Spiritual Friendship* in the form of a conversation among friends: Aelred and his fellow monks Ivo, Walter, and Gratian. Too, Aelred not only employs themes and ideas of friendship he found in Cicero but sometimes even takes passages from *De Amicitia* and incorporates them virtually verbatim into *Spiritual Friendship*.

Nonetheless, Aelred also wants to distance himself from the pagan philosopher to make it clear he is a different person now and is living in a different world, no longer at the court of King David but at the abbey of Rievaulx. He is telling a different story now because his primary aim in life is not to amass power at court, or wealth and fame, but to grow in charity and holiness by devoting his life to Christ and his brothers. Conversions change our estimation of what matters. They make us rethink things and spur reevaluations of nearly every aspect of our lives, including our relationships. In *Spiritual Friendship* the influence of Cicero is strong, but Aelred wants to make it clear that since his conversion he has moved beyond Cicero to a new and different understanding of friendship. He has come to think of friendship differently because he has grown to appreciate its importance for our life in Christ. Just as Augustine's views on friendship altered after his conversion, so did Aelred's.

Spiritual Friendship can seem quaint to us, but we should remember that it is written by a man whose life had been radically changed by Christ, so much so that it compelled Aelred to relocate his life from the Scottish court of King David to the cloister of Rievaulx. Aelred's charge now is not to enhance the political fortunes of his king or to plot his own career, but to guide his monks in their shared life of holiness. His aim is not to decipher court intrigues, but to fathom how to help the monks entrusted to him grow together in Christ. Too, Aelred realizes the world of Rievaulx is just as fallible and corruptible as the one he left behind. His brother monks may be striving for holiness, but often they stumble more than they soar. Sometimes he sees around him the same pettiness and pride he must have known at the court of King David. Monasteries, Aelred hints, may have their saints, but they also have their scoundrels. Just like royal palaces, they can be breeding grounds for gossip, jealousies, power plays, lingering grudges, and silly infatuations. This is the very human community to which Aelred writes. Knowing his and his brothers' weaknesses, he also knows they are nonetheless called together to Christ. So we can learn much about friendship from Aelred and can discover in him a very humane, wise, and holy man.

Three Kinds of Friendship and What They Mean

As I noted earlier, in his *Nichomachean Ethics* Aristotle identifies three kinds of friendships: friendships of usefulness or advantage, friendships of pleasure, and friendships of virtue or character. Even though he only considers virtue and character friendships to be friendships in the truest and most complete sense, Aristotle nonetheless sees value in the two lesser kinds of friendship and accepts them as both important and necessary in life. Like Aristotle, Aelred identifies three kinds of friendship, but unlike his Athenian predecessor, Aelred rejects the first two kinds of friendship and accepts only the third, *spiritual friendship*, as fulfilling all the requirements of friendship.

This may sound elitist, but we have to remember Aelred's purpose. His explicit concern is the place of friendship in the monastic life at Rievaulx and how friendships might help his fellow monks grow in their common vocation. He wants them to be able to discriminate among relationships by learning to distinguish relationships that are emotionally, psychologically, morally, and spiritually healthy from those that may seem emotionally appealing but are ultimately destructive. Aelred is a realist. He has seen all sorts of relationships and watched what they can do to people. He has seen people grow and flourish in healthy friendships, but he has also seen them become trapped in alliances that may have the appearance of friendship but that harm and diminish the friends.

Thus, he calls our attention to the first two kinds of friendship so we—and his brother monks—may see clearly the kinds of relationships we ought to avoid. These are relationships he has seen both at the court of King David and in the abbey at Rievaulx. These are relationships about which we need to be prudent and astute precisely because they can so easily attract us. Haven't most of us been in relationships we later came to sorely regret, but which initially seemed so promising? Didn't we at least once in our lives mistake the intensity of an infatuation for real love?

So before Aelred talks about spiritual friendship, he warns his fellow monks about other kinds of relationships that are not only detrimental to their community but are also morally and spiritually harmful. He gives extensive attention to the first two types of friendship because he knows how vulnerable his brother monks may be to them. He describes them in great detail because he wants them to see clearly both how easy it is to fall into such relationships and why we ought to avoid them. Aelred invites us to reflect on the different relationships of our lives and what they might be doing to us. He cautions us to be careful about the relationships we form and reminds us that not every relationship to which we give the name "friendship" may be a friendship at all.

The first type of friendship Aelred speaks about is carnal friendship. The very name shows what Aelred thinks of these relationships! How many of us would proudly boast that we had many carnal friendships? It could not be clearer that these are relationships to avoid. Carnal usually refers to anything having to do with the flesh, but Aelred uses the term in a much broader sense. Carnal friendships may involve sexual expression—and

some scholars believe there were some homosexual relationships among the monks at Rievaulx—but for Aelred they refer
to any relationships that originate in a mutual love for immoral-
ity. As we mentioned in chapter 2, true friendships are centered
around what is good, and true friends seek what is best for one
another. This is not possible in carnal friendships because carnal friendships, Aelred says, spring "from mutual harmony in
vice."[2] In these relationships, what attracts people to one another
is a sense of one another's weaknesses and the belief that not
only have they found a partner who will not challenge them to
change but also that with this person they can pursue what is
evil and remain undisturbed.

Carnal friendships are centered in shared weaknesses and
corrupting behavior. These "friends" play on one another's weaknesses and encourage each other in behaviors and ways of life
that are harmful. At their worst, then, carnal friendships are
partnerships in evil—sinful relationships in which a person has
found someone with whom he or she is comfortable doing
wrong. Such relationships can appear to be friendships because
the bond between such persons can be quite strong, but they fail
every test of friendship precisely because the cumulative effect
of carnal friendships is not to make one another better, but worse.

These are exactly the opposite of Aristotle's virtue friendships
or Augustine's theological account of friendship. Unlike virtue
friendships, the harvest of these twisted relationships is not
human flourishing but decline. People do not grow in carnal
friendships; they progressively diminish as they lose whatever
goodness and virtue they had. Moreover, such "friends" are the
last to realize what the relationship is doing to them because
carnal friendships feed on self-deception. Each person convinces
the other the relationship is good because the last thing they
want to hear from one another is the truth. Neither will challenge the other to change, neither will appeal to the other's
dimmed conscience or dwindling moral awareness, so they may
disastrously continue in their delusion until there is nothing left
of their souls but ashes.

Is Aelred unduly harsh? His account of carnal friendships
may leave us congratulating ourselves for never having fallen
into such abysmal relationships in our lives, but we should be
careful about dismissing him too quickly. What are the rela-

tionships we regret and why? If we took an inventory of all the relationships of our lives, what would it show us? Aelred's account of carnal friendships prompts us to think about the friendships of our lives and what they are doing to us. It challenges us to be honest about what the various relationships of our lives encourage in us. How are they marking us? Where are they taking us?

No matter what we call such relationships, we should never think of them as friendships. Carnal friendships are morally and spiritually debilitating because they encourage the worst in us, they make us comfortable with doing wrong, they deaden our consciences and destroy our moral sensitivity, they harden our hearts, and they turn us away from God. Such catastrophic consequences happen gradually, and that is what makes these relationships so dangerous. Nobody destroys his conscience all at once. Think about relationships where we grow comfortable with spreading rumors about others. Think about friends who do not challenge us when we say something malicious. Think about people who encourage us to ridicule others, or about those who make us comfortable in being selfish and exclusive. Have we ever known friends who are not bothered when we lie?

We might never think of such relationships as carnal friendships and might protest that they did not turn us away from God, but what then did they do to us? Is it possible to be in such relationships without being corrupted? Can we honestly say they did not change our character in ways we ought to regret? There are people whose presence in our lives has nurtured envy, jealousy, self-centeredness, anger, cynicism, bitterness, lust, or vindictiveness in us. There are those who have urged us into behavior of which we were later ashamed. Aelred warns us about such relationships because what they cultivate in us are not the virtues but the deadly sins.

These relationships really are not friendships at all for two reasons. First, true friendships should always make us better, not worse. Our friends should appeal to what is best in us and help us achieve our most magnanimous possibilities. This is not possible in carnal friendships. Second, as we mentioned in chapter 2, an essential mark of friendship is benevolence. Friends want what is best for one another and devote themselves to seeking and achieving it together, but there can be no true benevolence in relationships whose aim is not to help us achieve what is best but to make us comfortable with all that is corrupting. True friends help one another nurture a love for all that is good, but in carnal friendships the thing that is nurtured is not a love for virtue but a taste for vice.

Aelred begins his account on friendship with a clear and forceful rejection of such seductive but destructive relationships. He wants the monks of Rievaulx to know that carnal friendships are real possibilities in anyone's life. We should never honor these relationships with the name of friendship.

> Falsely do they claim the illustrious name of friends among whom there exists a harmony of vices; since he who does not love is not a friend, but he does not love his fellow-man who loves iniquity. "For he that loves iniquity" does not love, but "hates his own soul." Truly, he who does not love his own soul will not be able to love the soul of another. Thus it follows that they glory only in the name of friendship and are deceived by a distorted image and are not supported by truth (1:35–36).

The second kind of "friendship" Aelred discusses is *worldly friendships*. They appear better than carnal friendships but are nonetheless deficient because, Aelred says, they are born not from a desire for goodness but from a "desire for temporal advantage or possessions" (1:42). In fact, such friendships are "always full of deceit and intrigue." They "contain nothing certain, nothing constant, nothing secure," and change "with fortune and follow the purse" (1:42). In general, Aelred understands worldly friendships to be those relationships that nurture in us the wrong kinds of ambitions. Do we sometimes seek relationships with others only because of something we can gain from them? Have we ever sought to cultivate a friendship with a person because we felt doing so could advance us?

This is what Aelred is talking about. Worldly friendships are alliances we form with others that are essentially self-serving. What distinguishes them from true friendships is that in friendships that are genuine our focus is on the needs and well-being of the other, not ourselves. Since the purpose of worldly friendships is to achieve our own advantage, they are "full of deceit and intrigue" and are seldom long-lasting. If what motivates us to form relationships with others is simply how they might serve our purposes, the "friendships" will end as soon as they no longer do so. These are calculating, devious relationships that have the appearance of friendship because each "friend" will be a master at flattering the other, but beneath the flattery lies little affection or genuine regard. Indeed, the flattery may cover a barely concealed contempt.

Perhaps these were the kinds of relationships Aelred too often saw around him at the court of King David, but he likely witnessed them within the walls of Rievaulx as well—whenever he saw relationships developing that seemed more manipulative and self-serving than genuinely loving, or whenever he watched members of his community seeking relationships that might initially be quite intense and all-consuming but dissipated as soon as the needs of one or both were no longer being met. People primed for worldly friendships form them fast and end them quickly. They move from person to person, skilled as they are in discerning who will serve them best. With an eye always on the future, they seldom notice the harm they have done and the hurt they have left behind.

Where do we find these relationships today? Sadly, they can abound in business, in politics, in colleges and universities, and even in our churches. There is no shortage of people who plot how to achieve what is best for them regardless of the cost to others. We see this in the business world when people form connections that will help them get ahead but feel no remorse in betraying one another when the friendship is no longer advantageous. We see worldly friendships in politics when politicians flock to whomever seems in favor but abandon them the instant their fortunes change. We see worldly friendships in our churches when leaders who ought to be concerned about service become more interested in power, titles, and ecclesiastical rank.

What makes worldly friendships dangerous is that the evil at work in them is much more subtle than the evil of carnal friendships. It is hard to disguise what is corrupting about carnal friendships, but in our society today worldly friendships are not only admired and celebrated but often held up as something to which we should aspire. We admire the powerful. We worship our celebrities. We would love to be noticed as the famous are

noticed, and sometimes we would be willing to compromise ourselves if we could taste the success they have known.

But here is a twelfth-century monk warning us to be careful.
The dangers of cultivating worldly friendships are plentiful.
There is a superficiality and sterility to these relationships that
can quickly trivialize our lives. People who have worldly friendships have nothing, because these relationships have little depth
and little future. They are also rather safe relationships because
they ask nothing of us other than that we continue to put ourselves first, which is something we all know how to do pretty
well anyway. We won't grow in these relationships, and we will
never be challenged in them. True friendships develop us morally
and spiritually because in them we learn how to care for someone other than ourselves. They teach us how to see beyond our
own immediate needs and gratification by identifying with the
good of another. True friendships free us from the enervating
prison of self-centeredness, while worldly friendships deceive
us into believing we are most free when we look after ourselves
first. Most of all, any relationship that is driven by calculated
self-interest violates what a friendship ought to be about.

Aelred's analysis of worldly friendships counsels us to be wary
of certain ambitions that can conquer our hearts. For example,
if a desire for wealth drives all of our actions, we will find ourselves making choices we thought we would never embrace or
compromising ourselves in ways we will later regret. Similarly,
if a thirst for power takes hold of us, we may discover how easy
it is to use people who can help us get ahead or how skilled we
have become at rationalizing behavior we ought to repent. It is
notoriously easy for all of us to live "off center," and that is what
happens when we cultivate relationships whose sole purpose is
to satisfy our wayward ambitions. Worldly friendships are such
a part of the landscape of our world that we may hardly consider them worthy of moral reflection. No matter how we might
try to defend them, these relationships involve using another
human being strictly for our gain, and such disregard for the
dignity of another is always wrong.

Before we leave this discussion of the two kinds of relationships that Aelred believes are detrimental to our moral and spiritual development, one other point he makes is worthy of our
attention. Aelred reflects on the great influence friends have on

one another and how we sometimes use that influence to try to persuade our friends to do something they should not. We see this especially among adolescents, where peer pressure is great. We have likely heard stories of persons who have asked their friends to lie for them. I know people whose friends have asked them to steal for them. And anyone who teaches has probably heard instances where one student has asked another if she can submit the other's paper as if it were her own. But such violations of friendship are hardly limited to the young. Adults also abuse friendships if they manipulate their friends for unworthy ends or coerce them to do something that violates their conscience.

This is why Aelred says the greatest sin against friendship is to ask our friends to do anything sinful in the name of friendship. Nothing desecrates a friendship more than to use the influence we have with our friends to persuade them to do something wrong *because they are our friends*. Doing so shows no respect for either the friend or the friendship and is a terrible violation of the sacred trust that is the cornerstone of friendship.

Aelred mentions this because he appreciates how much friends try to please one another and honor each other's wishes. When our friends ask us to do something, we do not want to disappoint them because they are our friends and they matter to us. Saying no to a friend can make us feel we have failed the friendship. Because we trust our friends have our best interests at heart, we are reluctant to believe they would ever ask anything shameful of us. To do so is a horrible betrayal of the confidence we have in our friends and they have in us. This is why Aelred says a friend must be resolved "neither to ask others to do wrong nor to do wrong himself at another's request" (2:43). In short, we may not be able to trust everybody, but we surely ought to be able to trust our friends. In one of the more memorable passages from *Spiritual Friendship*, Aelred writes:

> For that love is shameful and unworthy of the name of friendship wherein anything foul is demanded of a friend; and this is precisely what one is forced to do, if, with vices in no wise dormant or subdued, he is either enticed or impelled to all sorts of illicit acts. Therefore, one ought to detest the opinion of those

who think that one should act in behalf of a friend in a way detrimental to faith and unrightness. For it is not excuse for sin, that you sin for the sake of a friend (2:39–40).

Like everything else in our lives, Aelred believes friendships should serve our life with God, never draw us away from God or separate us from God. One infallible way of evaluating the relationships of our lives is to ask ourselves if in them we are moving closer to God or falling further away. What is this friendship doing to me? Is it deepening my friendship with God or is it making me unmindful of God? Is it helping me grow morally and spiritually or is it developing attitudes and habits in me about which I ought to be concerned? Aelred wasn't being scrupulous or overly conscientious, but when he looked around him at Rievaulx he must have asked these questions when he pondered the relationships he saw among his brother monks. The best counsel he could give was to have them ask how their friendships were impacting their friendship with God. As he reminds the community at Rievaulx, no friendship should ever separate us from God by bringing about the death of our soul:

> Hence, since the life of the soul is of far greater excellence than that of the body, any action, we believe, should be altogether denied a friend which brings about the death of the soul, that is, sin, which separated God from the soul and the soul from life (2:69).

Spiritual Friendship: When Friendship is Life Together in Christ

If carnal friendships and worldly friendships risk separating us from God, there must be a better kind of friendship that can draw us closer to God, and for Aelred that is the purpose of *spiritual friendship*. Every friendship is formed around shared goods that identify the friendship and help the friends understand the life and purpose of the friendship. In spiritual friendship the principal good is a mutual love for Christ and a desire to grow together in Christ. This is what distinguishes spiritual friendships from other relationships. In spiritual friendships the

friends are centered in Christ, they seek Christ, and they strive
to live according to Christ. Through their friendship they want
to help one another live a godly and holy life. They want each
other to become resplendent in goodness.

Furthermore, Christ is a partner to every spiritual friendship.
Spiritual friendships always include more than two friends
because Christ is the "third" in the friendship, just as much present
to the friendship as the friends are to one another. For Aelred,
spiritual friendship is *life in and with Christ,* and *life for the sake
of Christ.* Moreover, the friends understand themselves to be living
together in Christ. In the opening sentence of *Spiritual
Friendship* Aelred makes this clear. He is speaking with his fellow
monk Ivo and says, "Here we are, you and I, and I hope a
third, Christ, is in our midst" (1:1). Later, Ivo puts it even more
strongly when he says, "However, I am convinced that true
friendship cannot exist among those who live without Christ"
(1:16). Remember that Aelred's concern is the spiritual lives of
the monks at Rievaulx. He wants them to have good and healthy
friendships but above all wants to be sure all their relationships
assist them in living more fully their Christian and monastic
vocations.

For Aelred, then, this is spiritual friendship, two or more people
coming together to pursue a life of seeking God *in Christ.*
Spiritual friendship is life together in Christ—that is its purpose
and rationale, its most basic activity. Spiritual friendships begin
in Christ, are understood to be an ongoing life in Christ, and are
perfected in Christ. This is why we can say spiritual friendship
is a *discipleship life,* a way in which people who are committed
to growing in Christ help one another imitate Christ and grow
in gospel virtues. Spiritual friends, through their life together,
learn from one another what discipleship means and how we
can acquire and develop the attitudes and virtues of Christ—
they help each other become better friends of God. As Aelred
writes, "And, a thing even more excellent than all these considerations,
friendship is a stage bordering upon that perfection
which consists in the love and knowledge of God, so that man,
from being a friend of his fellow man becomes the friend of God
. . ." (2:14). For Aelred, spiritual friendships represent the highest
possibility for any friendship because through them we "practice
our baptisms" by growing in Christ together. As he says,

For what more sublime can be said of friendship, what more true, what more profitable, than that it ought to, and is proved to, begin in Christ, continue in Christ, and be perfected in Christ (1:10).

Spiritual friendships are ways people who are intimate companions in the faith live out their baptisms and grow in Christ together. We need people with whom we can connect in faith. We need people who care enough for us not only to be interested in our spiritual well-being, but who also devote themselves to helping us achieve it. Isn't this a way of understanding the church? Should we not find in the church companions in faith, people who pledge to help one another "practice their baptisms" and grow in Christ together? Should not the Christian community be the one place where we find people who are committed to one another's spiritual well-being and who pledge to help each other grow in a gospel life? This is not to suggest every member of a congregation or parish must be intimate friends with *every* other member, but it is to say we ought to be able to find in the church a community of fellow disciples who care enough about each other's life in God that they can count on one another to help them live more faithfully.

Spiritual friends can be those special people in our lives with whom we can share the most intimate matters of soul, but they can also be the fellow believers who worship with us each week and who, like us, care deeply about the things of God. If, as we suggested in chapter 1, the worship and liturgy of the church should form us into a community of the friends of God, then can we not also say that through such worship we grow together in spiritual friendship and help one another in a gospel life? In this way spiritual friendship describes not only those singular people who draw us closer to God but is likewise a metaphor for the kind of community liturgy and worship should be making of us.

All this may make spiritual friendships sound like very serious business and not very much fun—something like medicine we know we have to take but that tastes awful when we take it. Spiritual friendships do focus on the most important calling of our lives, but this does not mean they are somber, joyless relationships. When spiritual friends get together they do not ask each other, "Well, how are your virtues today?" or "Well, how are you doing with the gospel life?" To have a spiritual friendship does not mean you do nothing but talk about holiness, Jesus, and the gospel, or that you are always comparing your virtues and mourning your faults.

A spiritual friendship is in some ways a unique relationship, but it is also in many ways a normal one. The friends do all sorts of things together, but they do them as spiritual friends, as people who know that whatever they might be doing, they are doing it *together in Christ*. They know Christ accompanies them wherever they go and that Christ is in their midst no matter what they might be doing. They can go to movies and plays together, they can spend an afternoon shopping or touring a museum, they can go to lunch or dinner, or simply take a walk together. Spiritual friends do all the things best friends do together, but they understand their friendship a particular way. They know what they hold in common, they know where their hearts are centered, and they know that what they want more than anything else in life is to deepen their friendship with God.

As they spend time together they not only learn about the spiritual life, they live it. They live it in the joy they share. They live it in learning to care for one another and in being faithful to one another. They live it when they pray together and when they are patient with one another. They live it when they offer each other advice and are not afraid to challenge one another. They live it when they make one another laugh and when they help one another hope. These are all central elements to the Christian life and aspects of spiritual friendship, and they suggest that spiritual friendships are not so rare and inaccessible that only a spiritual elite can enjoy them. No, spiritual friendships designate the relationships we have with those intimate friends who share our love for God and want, like us, to make of our life an *imitatio Christi*. We may never use the term "spiritual friendship" to describe the relationship and may not always explicitly discuss anything religious with these friends, but we know we learn more about God and goodness because of them, and when we are with them we know we are in the presence of a true disciple.

Friends: Why We Can't Leave Home Without Them

Aelred explores many aspects of friendship in *Spiritual Friendship*, but in addition to his discussion of the three types of friendship, he devotes much attention to why any human life is incomplete without friends. We have spoken of the importance of friendship in the Christian life, but there are other reasons, Aelred says, our lives will be lacking without good friends.

First, friendship is basic to our nature, a fundamental need at the heart of what it means to be human. This need is not something we have to create or cultivate; rather, it is something we cannot escape. We have a natural desire for friendships because it is our nature to need others and to live in relationship with them. A desire for friendship is one of our most basic and enduring inclinations, as inescapable as our need for food, drink, clothing, and shelter.

This is how Aelred interprets the Genesis story of the creation of the first human beings. The first story about human beings in the Bible is a story of our need for companionship. Unlike many who have interpreted the creation story of Adam and Eve as a parable for marriage, Aelred gives it a broader meaning. For Aelred, the creation story is not specifically about marriage, but about friendship. This is understandable since he was writing for a community of celibate monks, none of whom was to be married. But it is also revealing because to make the creation of the first human beings a parable of friendship suggests that from the beginning to be human is to stand in need of friendships. This need both defines and explains who human beings are. By interpreting the creation story of Adam and Eve as a story of friendship, Aelred argues there is no escaping our need for friendship. Just as Adam could not take up life without a partner, nor can we get on in life without friends. And just as Adam felt incomplete and lonely without the partnership of Eve, so does our humanity stand incomplete and stunted without relationships of friendship.

Friendship is a need we must satisfy—a fundamental condition of our nature—for an authentically human life to be possible. It is a need stitched into the fabric of creation indicating what being human requires and the sorts of relationships that will fulfill us. Indeed, to live in friendship is to live in deep harmony with our nature, but to be without friends or to have little understanding of what friendship is and requires, Aelred suggests, is to be caught in a life that cannot be fully human.

When Aelred looks closely at the Genesis story of the creation of the woman from the side of the man (Gen. 2:21–22), he says the very manner of creating the woman makes her a fitting friend for the man and the man a fitting friend for the woman. The fact that the woman was drawn from the side of the man indicates she is his equal in everything, and it is because of this that deep friendship, partnership, and affection are possible between them. If she was either too far superior to the man or too inferior, there could not be friendship because where differences are too extreme friendship is impossible. On the other hand, if she were not in some ways significantly different from the man, friendship would not be possible either because friendships require a balance of similarities and differences. As Aelred reads the Genesis story he sees the basic equality-in-difference between the man and the woman as what makes each fit for friendship with the other. In fact, the story reveals that friendships are not relationships of inequality and subordination, but of equality, mutuality, and reciprocal respect, and this is true whether the friendship is between a man and a woman or two men or two women. In words that may surprise us for a twelfth-century monk, Aelred says,

> How beautiful it is that the second human being was taken from the side of the first, so that nature might teach that human beings are equal and, as it were, collateral, and that there is in human affairs neither a superior nor an inferior, a characteristic of true friendship (1:57).

A second reason Aelred says we need good friendships is that life is often hard for us, more than any of us can handle alone. Aelred touches on something all of us know to be true. No matter how blessed we may be, eventually we face times of adversity and hardship. We experience not only disappointments and setbacks but sometimes terrible losses from which we are not sure we will ever recover. Too, no matter how hard we try to bring order and peace to our lives, there are moments when everything seems to be falling apart and times when we not only feel we are drowning but are sure someone or something is holding us under. None of us can navigate the perils of life alone, and we shouldn't try to do so. Sometimes we need to be rescued. Sometimes we need others to lean on, someone to take our hand and guide us along when our luck runs out, and this is what friends do for us. At moments of chaos and confusion, suffering and loss in our lives, they do not want us to be alone. They want to be with us and help us through our tribulations.

Think of the parable of the good Samaritan. There are times in our lives when we feel as if we have been robbed and beaten and left on the roadside to die. At such moments we know we could never survive without the support, consolation, and guidance of our friends. They are the good Samaritans who lift us up and carry us along when we are too weak and disheartened to do so ourselves. Life can bloody us, and when it does our friends are not afraid to bind up our wounds and walk with us as long as necessary for us to be healed and restored. It is their care, love, and compassion that strengthen us and help draw us back to life.

For Aelred, one sure mark of faithfulness is a friend's willingness to stand with us when doing so is difficult. We know who our good friends are by recounting the people who did not flee when life was hard for us or fall away when the darkness seemed much stronger than the light. Our friends are the people who are not reluctant to share in our sufferings and not afraid to be with us when we mourn. They see us through times of failure and are not ashamed to stand by us when others judge and abandon us. This is why Aelred, echoing the Book of Sirach, speaks of friendship as "the medicine of life," a tonic for all that might befall us.

"A friend," says the Wise Man, "is the medicine of life" (Sir. 6:16). Excellent, indeed, is that saying. For medicine is not more powerful or more efficacious for our wounds in all our temporal needs than the possession of a friend who meets every misfortune joyfully, so that, as the Apostle says, shoulder to shoulder, they bear one another's burdens. Even more—each one carries his own injuries even more lightly than that of his friend. Friendship, therefore, heightens the joys of prosperity and mitigates the sorrows of adversity by dividing and sharing them. Hence, the best medicine in life is a friend (2:12–13).

A third reason we need friendships is that each of us needs someone with whom we can be completely open, someone with whom we can *relax our heart*. We need someone we trust and feel comfortable enough with to share the secrets, dreams, and hopes of our hearts, including matters of the soul. We need a soulmate, a confidant who cares enough for us and respects us so completely that we do not fear revealing to him or to her the deepest parts of who we are, even those aspects of our lives of which we might be embarrassed or ashamed: our failures and fears, our struggles and ongoing temptations, even our sinfulness. We need someone with whom we are able *to speak our soul*, confident that they will not betray our trust. Our best friends, especially spiritual friends, are the people with whom we do not hesitate to share whatever is in our heart.

Aelred describes spiritual friends as those with whom we share "all our confidences and plans" (3:83). This is what distinguishes spiritual friendships from the other relationships of our lives and makes them such a treasure. There may be many for whom we feel goodwill and affection, and many whose company we enjoy, but we would hesitate to entrust to them the deepest secrets of our lives, especially our spiritual lives. As Aelred says, we may care for these people, but "it would be imprudent to lay bare our souls and pour out our inner hearts" (3:84) to them. We should "bare our souls" only to those we are certain want what is best for us, know us better than most, and would never betray us, which is why Aelred says we should "not form intimacies too quickly" (3:40). Our best friends, and for Aelred our spiritual friends, are the people—probably few—with whom we are willing to confide everything. As he writes,

> But what happiness, what security, what joy to have someone to whom you dare to speak on terms of equality as to another self; one to whom you need have no fear to confess your failings; one to whom you can unblushingly make known what progress you have made in the spiritual life; one to whom you can entrust all the secrets of your heart and before whom you can place all your plans! (2:11)

One of the great joys of spiritual friendship is the depth of sharing that can occur between the friends, but it is important to note that this sharing has a purpose that is more spiritual than therapeutic. One of the gifts of spiritual friendship is that the friends help one another deepen in Christlike love and overcome barriers to holiness in their lives. The purpose of their friendship is not necessarily to make one another feel good but to help one another be good. This is why we must allow these friends to offer us counsel, guidance, and even challenge and correction as we struggle to grow in Christ. Spiritual friendships are relationships built not on flattery but the truth. These friends help one another seek what is morally and spiritually excellent. They even help one another with their sins and imperfections. Most important, they are not afraid to speak if they see one another slipping into behavior that will harm their relationship with Christ and draw them away from God.

Spiritual friends do not see us changing in ways that are harmful and keep silent. They are willing to be truthful with us because they care for us and do not want us to imperil the most promising possibility of our lives: our friendship with God. Such friends are rare because it takes courage to speak the truth when doing so risks our being misunderstood or rejected by another. It is much easier to flatter our friends than be truthful with them, and one of the dangers in any friendship is that we begin consoling one another with comforting deceptions instead of challenging one another with the truth. Despite our protests, often we do not want to hear the truth from our friends. Perhaps we have ended friendships when friends cared enough about us to tell us the truth; but if we flee friendships every time our friends speak an uncomfortable truth, none of our relationships can help us grow because all of them will be safely superficial.

At the same time, if spiritual friends can speak the truth to one another, it is only because they know how deeply committed they are to one another. We are much less likely to speak or hear the truth if we question the stability of a relationship or the faithfulness of a friend. One sure sign that relationships are in trouble, whether it be in friendship, marriage, or community life, is when people suspect the relationships are not strong enough to bear the truth. If we suspect the foundations of a relationship are fragile, we will say anything but the truth because we fear the truth will only expose how frail the relationship really is. In such situations people can be cheerful and friendly to one another, and to outside observers seem full of care for one another, but they have an unspoken agreement never to be completely truthful with one another because they know the bond of their relationship is so threadbare that the weight of the truth would snap it.

Good friends not only are truthful with one another, but they also stand by one another when the truth that is spoken is painful. For instance, good friends do not abandon us when we are struggling with the shortcomings, weaknesses, and imperfections of our lives. They help us through these times precisely because they are truthful with us and care for us. There are chapters in any lifelong friendship when the friends help one another with moral and spiritual rehabilitation. There are times in any seasoned friendship when one of the friends has to be patient with the other's failures, sometimes egregious failures, and help them recover their integrity. To abandon our friends when they are struggling would suggest we had given up on them and did not believe they could change. To leave when their lives are in pieces would suggest we had lost hope in them and no longer found them worthy of love. *Friends do not give up on one another.*

Take the example of Sister Helen Prejean, the nun whose work with inmates on death row became famous in *Dead Man Walking.* Sr. Helen never denied the horrible evils committed by these men, but neither did she deny they remained creatures made in the image and likeness of God. She could be honest about their terrible failures and still have hope for them because she never failed to see them as children of God, even when they made it immensely difficult to do so.

The poet Lord Byron said, "Friendship is love without wings." A friend does not flee at the first sign of trouble or difficulty in our lives, but stands fast with us in love. If they do, it is only because, like Sr. Helen Prejean, they are able to see something more in us than our failures and defeats. True, they see our weaknesses and abundant imperfections, but they also see something immensely more important and promising about us, namely our undying potential to love and serve God, to give ourselves for others, to grow in holiness and goodness, and to become one with the Christ to whom we joined our lives at baptism.

What does this mean for the church, the community of the friends of God? Aelred's analysis of spiritual friendship challenges our churches to become communities where people help one another overcome barriers to holiness and grow in Christ-like love. If this sounds strange to us—even impossibly utopian—perhaps it is because so many of our churches are like the safe and superficial relationships where people become experts at flattery because they are afraid of the truth. Churches should be places where our common life in Christ enables us to speak the truth to one another, to counsel, challenge, and even correct one another. This happens in few places today because in so many churches we gather as strangers, worship as strangers, and leave as strangers. It happens because we love our isolation and do not want anyone, even a sister or brother in Christ, to know us well enough to speak the unflattering word.

We want no one trespassing on our hearts, but the church ought to be the place where we welcome such trespassers whenever their intrusions can awaken us from our slumbers and draw us closer to God. Such a community ought to be created through the prayer and worship of the church. If we worship dangerously, we will become a community where nobody is shocked when the faults and failures of everyone become glaringly transparent. Such epiphanies will not shatter the community because the love of Christ that makes them one is so much deeper, so much more resilient.

Christian Friendships and the Reign of God

This chapter has been a conversation with a medieval monk, Aelred of Rievaulx. He scrutinized friendship because he wanted to instruct his brothers on how their friendships could serve and enrich their lives in Christ and deepen their monastic vocation. We can learn from Aelred because what he says has implications far beyond the cloister walls of Rievaulx. His insights into the perils of relationships that appear to be friendships but are actually quite harmful remain timely. His account of the reasons why no life can be considered good without friendships not only reminds us of the priceless treasure good friends are but also why we should never take them for granted.

Still, for Christians, friendships have a purpose far beyond one's own moral and spiritual development. Every friendship should make our world bigger, and Christian friendships should link us to the kingdom of God. Ultimately, the purpose of friendship in the church is not primarily our mutual edification but to make us the kind of community that can faithfully enact God's narrative of love, healing, and redemption in the world. If God has befriended us, how are we to befriend the world? If God has served us faithfully, how are we to serve others, particularly those who may not know God? One way is for the church, the friends of God, to be the community that embodies and exemplifies virtues that can transform the world in hope. What some of those virtues might be and how the church is called to live them will be the subject of the final three chapters.

six

Astounding Them by Our Way of Life

What Friends of God Can Offer the World

In a homily on 1 Corinthians, John Chrysostom, fourth-century theologian and renowned preacher, exhorts his congregation to win over the unbelievers in their midst not by the force of weapons, nor by wordy arguments, but by the overpowering witness of their lives:

> Let this, I say, be our way of overpowering them, and of conducting our warfare against them; and let us, before all words, astound them by our way of life. For this is the main battle, this is the unanswerable argument, the argument from actions. For though we give ten thousand precepts of philosophy in words, if we do not exhibit a life better than theirs, the gain is nothing. For it is not what is said that draws their attention, but their enquiry is, what we do. . . . Let us win them therefore by our life.[1]

This is one of the most insightful and challenging descriptions of how Christians should see themselves in the world. John Chrysostom reminds us of the power we have. It is not a power of weapons, or a power of wealth, riches, status, or prestige. It is not a power of subtle philosophies or wordy arguments; rather, it is the power of a holy, gracious, joyful, and hopeful way of life. The greatest power we as Christians have today—and have always had—is our faithful, heartfelt witness to a graced way of life.

We continue to reflect today on the role and relevance of religion and the churches in our world, but what Chrysostom reminds us is that there is nothing more important that we are called by God to do than to astound the world by our way of life. Our primary social responsibility is not to be Democrat or Republican, liberal or conservative, but to be a people who astound others by the goodness, truthfulness, justice, mercy, peace, and joy they see in us. As Chrysostom said, "Let us win them by our life."

The Christian life is completed in mission, in what the theologian Vigen Guroian calls "a holy ministry to the world."[2] This is what *Lumen Gentium,* the Second Vatican Council's Constitution on the Church, meant when it said all Christians have the mission of proclaiming and establishing the kingdom of God[3] and of being "instruments of salvation" and "visible sacraments of Christ"[4] in the world. These are not special tasks reserved for an elite but ought to be how all the baptized envision their lives in the world. We should be asking ourselves when we get up each morning, "For whom am I going to be an instrument of salvation today?" At home, at work, in our everyday interactions with others we should ask, "What is my holy ministry for today? How am I called to be a visible sacrament of Christ today?"

Every baptized Christian is entrusted with a mission. Our mission is to carry on the ministry of Jesus through the witness and character of our lives. Every baptized Christian is an apostle, one sent on a mission of proclaiming the gospel in word, deed, and action in their everyday lives. Baptism is not only for our personal sanctification but also for the ongoing sanctification of the world. So one of the most fitting ways for Christians to continue the mission and ministry of Jesus is by becoming a *virtuous community,* a community whose witness is measured in the promising distinctiveness of its life. These virtues should be learned and cultivated through the worship and liturgy of the church and through the everyday lives of its members. These virtues constitute what it means practically to live as a community of the friends of God in our world today. No list of such virtues would be complete, but some virtues seem especially urgent if our society is to know the liberation and freedom that comes in Christ. In this chapter we shall discuss two of these virtues: the virtue of truthful and reverent vision and the virtue and practice of being a people of hope.

The Virtue of Truthful and Reverent Vision

A story may help us understand the virtue of truthful and reverent vision and why it is so important. Several years ago I was in North Carolina and met a priest, a man in his early seventies, who talked with me about an afternoon he had spent in a shopping mall and why he came home distressed. After walking around the mall for awhile, he sat down to rest. And as he sat, he watched the people passing by and looked into their faces. What struck him was that in the faces of so many people, young as well as old, he did not see kind eyes. He did not see a compassionate, merciful, or benevolent look but often a hardened, threatening gaze. He saw coldness. He wondered how people saw the world through those eyes. How did they *see* other human beings? Did they see them humanely? Did they see them as gifts, as blessings of God? Or did they see them as nuisances and obstacles, even as enemies? Did they see them at all? He wondered too how they saw an aging man like himself, a man who increasingly depended on the help and kindness of others. Did they have the moral vision that would enable them to be thoughtful, compassionate, gracious, patient, and kind? These questions were important to him because he knew that if we fail to see other human beings through "kind eyes," all sorts of harm become possible.

This story reminds us of the importance of vision in the Christian life. Vision is a neglected quality in our moral and spiritual formation, but it is absolutely crucial. Normally we do not connect ethics and spirituality with learning to see. Instead, we parse morality in the language of rules and principles and obligations, or perhaps the language of character and virtue. When we talk of spirituality, so often we turn inward to examine the condition of our hearts before God. All of that is important, but it is not enough, and it may not be where we should begin a discussion of the Christian moral and spiritual life. As the late philosopher and novelist Iris Murdoch reminded us, how we act in a situation largely depends on how we see it.[5] There is an intrinsic connection between truthful vision and virtuous actions because we cannot *act rightly* unless we first *see rightly*. However, as Murdoch emphasized and a life of discipleship makes clear, seeing truthfully and reverently demands a lot more than just opening our eyes, because we can open our eyes and fail to really see.

For instance, if our vision is not reverent and truthful, our behavior will not be just. We will not see the bond we share with every human being as a child of God and the responsibilities that flow from that bond. If we look at the world through a vision skewed by self-serving fantasies—through a lens of self-centeredness and arrogance—our behavior is bound to do harm because, albeit perhaps unconsciously, we see everything in terms of our own needs and preferences. Our actions will lack compassion, kindness, justice, and love because we will not see the image of God in others, much less the inherent goodness and beauty in all of life. Or if we gaze upon the world through eyes of anger and resentment, or through a vision twisted by cynicism, our behavior will likely be thoughtless and rough, destined more to hurt than to bless. That will be the case not because we intentionally wish to do harm but because we lack the moral vision requisite for goodness.

We can appreciate the force of Murdoch's insight if we reflect on what it is like to live or work with someone who gazes upon the world through eyes of anger and resentment. All of their behavior is shaped by the belief that they have been unjustly slighted and denied. Or what happens to the person whose vision is characterized by bitterness and cynicism? Everything they do is born from a desire to strike back and to hurt. As Murdoch observed, "I can only choose within the world I can see."[6] What if our vision feeds on the toxins of jealousy, envy, arrogance, or greed? If our behavior turns on the quality of our perceptions, what if we perceive the world through eyes of lust, whether it be a lust for power, riches, prestige, or pleasure?

Every act of cruelty, every expression of injustice, every demeaning joke, and every prejudicial thought, attitude, word, or action is rooted in a failure of vision, an inability or refusal to see the God-given dignity and goodness of another human being. Without truthful and reverent vision, we will not see the sacredness and beauty of every man and woman as a child of God destined for friendship with God.

There is a movie called *The Elephant Man*. It is the story of a gentle, thoughtful, and sensitive Englishman who had the soul of an artist but who was also physically deformed. For much of his life he suffered the taunts and ridicule of people who came to see him as a circus sideshow attraction. He was seen and treated not as a human being, a child of God, but as a grotesque animal. Most people saw only his physical deformity, not the beauty and goodness of his soul. There is a scene in the movie where he is being chased by some bullying youths through the streets of London. He runs into a restroom in a park, trembling and terrified. The young men chasing him mock him, shove and push him, and throw rocks at him, but never once think of him as human. Backed up against a wall in the restroom, he suddenly turns to them and says from the depths of his soul, "I am not an animal! I am not an elephant! I am a human being!" He was letting them know he was not as they saw him, that there was a goodness and sacredness and dignity to him that was there whether they saw it or not.

The sad fact is that oftentimes we do not want to see. There is a stubborn tendency in all of us to illusion and distortion. We are called to see all human beings (and nonhuman creation as well) as the handiwork of God and to respond to them in love, but that is a high moral achievement, not a natural aptitude. So often we do not see things as they really are but as we need them to be. Instead of reverencing the world and responding to all things with justice and compassion, we twist everything to meet our needs. Instead of respecting other people and fulfilling our obligations toward them, we manipulate them to fit our plans and call this manipulation love. The world in all its mystery and goodness is hidden from us—its beauty easily missed—because our vision is neither transparent nor clear, but clouded by anxiety, deception, and self-interest. This is why Murdoch says the basic moral challenge is to "pierce the veil of selfishness" in order to see the world as it really is.[7] We cannot become good until we learn to see rightly, but this is a nettlesome challenge for all of

us because, at least occasionally, fantasy is stronger than the
truth.

Murdoch describes fantasy as "the proliferation of blinding
self-centered aims and images," and suggests it is often what
masters our hearts.[8] "Objectivity and unselfishness are not natural to human beings,"[9] she insists, as witnessed in our chronic
inability to see, much less respect, the beauty and goodness of
all creation. Our fantasizing tendencies run deep and breed endless illusions and misperceptions that are meant to console and
reassure us but that leave us living dangerously at odds with
reality. Obvious candidates for fantasy in our society today are
the ideologies of consumerism and materialism, ideologies of
power, ideologies of racism and sexism, our dangerous linking
of identity with self-assertion, our endless fascination with violence, and our foolish and costly thoughtlessness toward the
earth itself.

Whether they are the results of anxiety, fear, insecurity, selfishness, or simply the desire for power and control, the twisted
and self-serving visions of fantasy characterize persons and institutions that bend the world to themselves. Instead of seeing others as something to reverence and respect, persons and institutions trapped in fantasy see everything—other people, creation,
all of life—in reference to themselves and their needs. Fantasy
is manipulative and self-serving and always results in injustice
and harm. It is not fantasy we need but enlightenment, not more
deceit and delusions but reverent and truthful ways to see.

Think of the movie *Schindler's List*. There is a scene in the
movie where the German officer in charge of the labor camp,
Amon Goeth, is alone with a young Jewish woman, Helen
Hirsch, who works as a maid at his villa inside the camp. Amon
is attracted to her, but his attraction scares him because to be
drawn to Helen, a Jew, is to recognize her not as someone des-
picable and discardable but as a human being like himself. In
this scene he looks into her eyes and his own eyes are opened.
For a brief moment the truth breaks through and he sees her
not as vermin, not as some cancerous appendage on the body
of Germany, but as a human being. He sees past the demonic
fantasies of Nazism to glimpse her beauty and her goodness.
Amon Goeth has his epiphany, his revelatory moment, when
the scales fall from his eyes and he no longer sees the young

woman as someone to hate and possibly kill but as someone
like himself.

The truth scares him. *He is afraid to see*. He knows if he accepts
this new way of seeing Helen, his entire life will have to change.
If he lets this truthful, reverent vision of her take hold, he will
have to renounce the horrible lies of Nazism and repent. He cannot bear this truth and its ramifications. What he should do is
repent all the evil he has done and beg the young woman's forgiveness. But he cannot live with what he sees, so instead of asking her forgiveness and living in this new light, he beats her.
Instead of contrition and repentance, there is violence.

A very important virtue for us to cultivate today is the virtue
of reverent and truthful vision. There are many ways we can
describe this virtue. We can speak of it as a kind and compassionate stance toward life. We can speak of it as a loving and
merciful gaze toward all that lives. We can think of it as the spiritual ability to see and appreciate the inherent value in everything, not just other human beings but all of life. Reverence is
the fundamental moral attitude by which we relate to other
human beings and all of creation with care, kindness, thoughtfulness, patience, and compassion.[10] The reverent person knows
every individual and every creature deserves attentive respect.
She or he knows there is a beauty, goodness, and sacredness to
life we do not create but are called to honor. Such a person especially knows that without reverent and truthful vision we miss
so much of the goodness and beauty around us, whether it be
the smile on another person's face, the sometimes stunning
beauty of a flower, or the needy person reaching out to us for
help.

If part of our holy ministry to the world today is to be a people of truthful and reverent vision, how do we overcome our own
tendencies to fantasy and distortion in order to see the world
through the eyes of Christ? Virtuous action hinges on truthful
seeing, but acquiring a reverent and truthful vision is hardly
easy; indeed, it is essentially an *ascesis*, a demanding and sometimes daunting discipline by which we break through the deceptions and illusions of our lives so that we can see everyone and
everything "more clearly, more justly."[11] As Craig Dykstra writes,
"To act fittingly and responsibly is to act in response to truthful seeing, a seeing that peers into the mysterious depths of the

world and requires long discipline, patient effort, and the continuous shaping of the whole self by what is real."[12]

What Dykstra describes is what Christians have long called *contemplation.* Sometimes we can think of a contemplative as a person who withdraws from the world, but the true contemplative is not a person who pulls back from the world. The true contemplative is the person who commits to practicing new and better ways of seeing. In Dykstra's language, the contemplative is the person whose vision, whose whole way of being, is shaped by what is real. The contemplative is the person who wants to *see things as they really are in themselves* because he or she knows seeing is essential to goodness. What empowers us to break the hold of fantasy and see truthfully is an "attention to reality inspired by, consisting of, love,"[13] and that is exactly what contemplation is: the ongoing, sometimes arduous discipline by which we gradually overcome distorted and inadequate ways of seeing in order to see everything through a vision inspired not by selfishness or arrogance but love.

The fact is that "everything about us asks for our attention,"[14] but only the truly contemplative recognize this and know how to respond. Contemplation changes our customary ways of seeing. Through the discipline of contemplation our normal sense of perception, indeed our whole orientation to reality, is altered. Think of what happens when we allow ourselves to be drawn inside a Gospel parable. The power of a parable is to turn our usual ways of seeing and thinking upside down. Everything gets turned around inside a parable so that custom and convention are not only called into question but also *revealed as lacking.* The parable works to free us from false ways of seeing and to teach us to see not only differently and more imaginatively but also according to the revolutionary vision of the reign of God.

Contemplation can happen in all kinds of ways, not only through the biblical text. We need to be attuned to the revelatory moments of our everyday lives. We can learn the practice of contemplation when we look into the face of another human being, when we serve the poor, when we care for the sick or keep vigil with the dying, when we watch children play, when we stand before a beautiful painting or watch lightning split the sky. All these things can open our eyes and teach us to see. Again, contemplation does not entail turning our backs on the world;

rather, it is entering more deeply and truthfully into the beauty
and complexity of reality. It is the attentiveness that enables us
to see, love, and respect all that God has made and, therefore,
to live justly.

Here is an example of such a contemplative moment. A few
years ago I was flying from Chicago to San Antonio, a flight of
roughly three hours. It was early Saturday morning and I was
tired from too short a night. As I sat in my seat, a novel firmly
in hand, I watched the other passengers boarding and noticed
a family of three coming down the aisle: Mom, Dad, and a baby
of about six months. Like many airline passengers I began to
pray, "Dear Lord, please don't let that baby sit near me!" But
God does not always answer our prayers in the way we would
like, and sure enough this trio of fearsome passengers sat down
right in front of me. I clenched, knowing it would likely be a long
and woeful flight, and started to read my novel. About halfway
into the flight I had all but forgotten about this threatening child
until I looked up and noticed that the father was holding him
on his shoulder and that the baby, hardly more than six inches
away from me, was staring right at me and smiling. I started to
laugh because I felt that God, through this child, was saying,
"Wadell, don't take yourself so seriously. Learn to lighten up like
this child."

That is how we learn to see, and it can happen in so many
unexpected ways. Contemplative moments occur whenever
something startles us out of our usual ways of seeing and shows
us how poorly we have been seeing and how self-serving our
vision often is. Contemplative moments occur when employers
see their employees not as "resources" but as colleagues and
human beings. They happen when teachers see their students
not as tuition-paying customers or unfortunate distractions but
as gifts entrusted to them. They happen when church leaders
see people who question, critique, and sometimes disagree not
as turncoat dissenters but as members of the people of God who
care about the church as much as those who lead it.

There are other ways Christians learn to see. One obvious
context for gradually breaking free of our blindness and learning to see ought to be the liturgy and worship of the church. All
of us look at the world through certain images, symbols,
metaphors, and narratives. Our perceptions are framed and

shaped by an array of images that construct our view of reality and our understanding of our relationship to other people and the world. But in a culture that teaches us not to see and that in so many ways dulls our awareness of the inherent value in all life, where do we find symbols, images, metaphors, and narratives that will purify our vision and teach us how to live more compassionately and responsibly? Where do we find new images, symbols, metaphors, and narratives stunning enough to disorient us from our usual patterns of perception so that our whole way of seeing and being can be transformed?

We find them foremost in the Scriptures, in the biblical books Christians believe constitute a new and definitive *revelation*. In *Vision and Character*, Craig Dykstra says "the function of revelation is to provide us with images by which to see truthfully and realistically."[15] He speaks of revelation as those images, symbols, metaphors, and narratives that "help us to see more deeply and clearly into the world; they do not hide it from us or distort it"; rather, revelation helps us "to see . . . that we had not been able to see before."[16]

How might this happen? How do the Scriptures help us to see *that we had not been able to see before?* There are countless examples. Consider the story in Luke 7:36–50. Jesus is invited to dinner at the home of a well-known Pharisee. A woman "known in the town to be a sinner" anoints Jesus' feet with perfume and wipes them with her hair. The host is scandalized, claiming that if Jesus were truly a prophet and a man of God, he would know "who and what sort of woman this is that touches him—that she is a sinner." But whose vision is twisted? Jesus sees the woman not through harshness and judgment but through love. He sees her not as a worthless outcast of God but as one whose love, despite her sins, is great. If we listen to this story when we gather as a community in worship, how does it challenge and transform our own practices of seeing? Where does it suggest we need to purify how we see certain individuals or groups in our lives? Does it call us to repentance because perhaps, like the Pharisee in the story, there are times we see others less than graciously, zeroing in on their faults instead of acknowledging their love?

Or consider the famous miracle of the multiplication of the loaves and fishes, a miracle recounted in each of the four

Gospels, even twice in the Gospel of Matthew (Matt. 14:13–21; 15:32–38; Mark 6:34–44; Luke 9:10–17; John 6:1–13). In the story, Jesus has been followed by a "vast throng" who have been listening to him preach. Near the end of the day Jesus sees the tired and hungry crowd and tells his disciples to give them something to eat. The disciples say it is hopeless because the only food available belongs to a child, a young boy, and all he has are "five loaves and a couple of fish," hardly enough to feed a few, much less a crowd of thousands. But Jesus *sees differently*. He sees not that food is lacking but that there is more than enough for everyone if, being grateful to God for what we have, we are willing to share. The miracle of the loaves and fishes becomes a parable of economics reminding us that in the reign of God we are summoned not to abide by an economics of scarcity but by an economics of gratitude and generosity.

Shouldn't this be what the worship and liturgy of the church, particularly the Eucharist, teaches us? Shouldn't we learn that everything is a gift and that everything lives only because of the extravagant and ceaseless generosity of God?[17] Liturgy and worship should teach us to see and to live *eucharistically* so that through giving thanks for everything we change from plundering the goods of the earth and hoarding what we have to sharing.

Truthful and reverent vision is inseparable from worship because it is there that we encounter, listen to, and learn from the one we believe is the "true light," the one in whom we find the light that shatters all darkness. In him we learn to conform our lives not to the distortions of the present age but to the illuminating goodness of God. More than a few of Jesus' miracles have him restoring the sight of those who cannot see. In the touching story of the blind beggar Bartimaeus (Mark 10:46–52), Jesus calls him over and asks, "What do you want me to do for you?" Bartimaeus answers, "Rabboni, I want to see." His desire should be our desire. When we gather in worship we should pray, "Lord, teach us to see." We should pray that by listening to the Scriptures, particularly the stories of Jesus, and by opening ourselves to receive the Word that comes to us in the body and blood of Christ, our vision might be healed so that we can be a people, a community in the world, who see truthfully and graciously and, therefore, live justly and compassionately.

If we are to practice a holy ministry in the world today, we must commit ourselves to developing a truthful and reverent vision; we must see through the eyes of Christ. There is so much hardness in our world today, so much casual cruelty and thoughtlessness, so many ways people are desensitized, and it all reflects a failure in vision, the triumph of darkness over the light. One very important way for the church to serve the world is for it to be a community where people learn to see, where people learn justice, love, compassion, and reverence for life because they see everything resplendent with the goodness of God.

The Virtue and Practice of Being a People of Hope

A second virtue that urgently needs to be embodied and witnessed by the church today is hope. Hope is an essential virtue for life because without hope we cannot continue on our journey to fulfillment in God. We cannot live without hope because hope, along with patience and courage, fortifies us in dealing with all the challenges and adversities of life. Hope is easily lost as the tribulations of life mount, when we lose any sense of life's purpose, when we find ourselves increasingly distracted and bored, and, perhaps most of all, when we feel we are navigating life alone. It is exactly the necessity but precariousness of hope that makes it so important for the church, the friends of God, to be a "dwelling place of hope."

There is a scene in Jon Hassler's novel *North of Hope* that captures the frightening fragility of hope. As the title suggests, for many characters in the novel, hope seems out of reach, too far beyond their ordinary everyday experiences to be graspable. They live not in the warm center of hope that expresses itself in an energy and enthusiasm for life but in the frozen, barren landscape of sadness and despair. The novel is peopled with characters struggling to get by, stumbling through life with no more of a goal than trying to survive another day. They try to replace their lost hope with drugs and alcohol, with casual sex, with hours passed before the television, using all those things to numb the despair and emptiness of their lives. Hassler suggests hope is never something we can take for granted because so many things in life wear it down. Hope is a fragile possession, something we must work hard to hold on to day after day.

One of the key scenes in the novel takes place in a unit of a psychiatric hospital.[18] It is called "Hope Unit," and it is where people whose lives are in pieces come to be healed and try to recover their hope. In this scene an elderly woman who is a patient in Hope Unit talks to Frank, a priest visiting the hospital. She tells him she had been feeling bad for ten years but did not think she was having a nervous breakdown. It never occurred to her she might be losing hope or that her life was falling apart. She just felt bad, a little depressed and scattered. But her little depression, stretched over ten years, led to a nervous breakdown, and on Christmas morning, a day that ought to be a feast of hope, she checked into the hospital. Through this story Hassler suggests we don't lose hope all at once. Hope erodes inch by inch, a little at a time, until one day we realize we have no hope.

This can happen in many ways. We work hard for what we believe in but nothing seems to change. We commit ourselves to what we think is a beautiful and noble dream but receive little support or encouragement and sometimes much opposition. Hope leaks out when people lose jobs they thought were secure and experience rejection and self-doubt. Single parents lose hope as they struggle to meet all the obligations and responsibilities of their lives and wonder if they will ever not be exhausted. Young people can lose hope if adults have not given them anything worth believing in, or if they believe the future is not very promising. All of us lose hope when we battle institutions that seem more against us than for us.

We may live in a culture of optimism, but we do not live in a culture of hope. Hope is the virtue that orients us to fulfillment, the virtue by which we seek, despite hardships and discouragements, our utmost possibilities in life. For Christians, hope is the truly theological virtue, rooted in grace, by which we turn our lives toward God and each day seek God and happiness with God.[19] It is through hope, Josef Pieper suggests, that we never give up on God's great promises to us. Hope, he writes, is the "steadfast orientation toward a fulfillment and a beatitude that are not 'owed'" us, but that God in his goodness has promised us, namely, "a real, grace-filled participation in the divine nature. . . ."[20] Hope is empowered by a vision, the vision of our most promising possibility of intimate union with God and all the saints.

If hope is the virtue by which we turn our lives toward God, this means every human life takes the form of a pilgrimage. We are pilgrims on a journey to the kingdom of God, pilgrims called to be part of God's great adventure and to share completely in the love, goodness, and joy of God. Pieper calls this our *status viatoris*, the "'condition or state of being on the way.'"[21] We live oriented toward absolute fulfillment in God, but as creatures "on the way" who are not yet fully with God. It is this tension between the "not yet" and the promise, between our orientation toward fulfillment and our imperfect possession of it, that makes hope necessary. In fact, Pieper calls hope "the virtue of the *status viatoris;* it is the proper virtue of the 'not yet.'"[22] Too, he contrasts the *status viatoris* with the *status comprehensoris,* the condition of one "who has comprehended, encompassed, arrived."[23] Short of the kingdom of God, no human being fully comprehends the love and goodness of God or can completely possess the beatitude of God, and it is this radical incompleteness, coupled with the inevitable disappointments and discouragements of life, that makes hope necessary but sometimes fragile. We may be anchored in a promise that assures us of fulfillment, but hardships in life can make that promise seem not only distant but unreachable, and at such moments our hearts can feel not the warmth of hope but the chill of despair.

This is a terrible possibility and one we have to take quite seriously. It is not farfetched to think that many people feel in their hearts more the lure of nothingness than the pull of hope. We meet these people in the workplace. We can find them in our churches. We may even live with them. They may be cheerful and friendly, but for too long sadness has ruled their hearts. They function in life, they are often quite busy, but they have known dejection and desolation more than contentment and have lost all hope of recovering joy. They have abandoned any sense of life as promising and are reluctant to believe any talk of a human being's vocation to find peace and fulfillment in God. For reasons we cannot always understand, and in ways of which they may hardly be aware, they anticipate each day "the non-fulfillment of hope."[24]

This is why there has to be a community that embodies hope. Christians do not believe having hope is easy, but they do believe hope corresponds to the innermost truth of who we are. If, as the Book of Wisdom says, "God fashioned all things that they might be," then despite the temptation of despair and the seduction of hopelessness, the truest law of our being is our deep and abiding inclination to life, the almost indelible desire to live. We cannot wash away this desire. We can deny it, repress it, and live in foolish contradiction to it, but we cannot ultimately silence the most fundamental grace and truth of our nature: God wants us to live. As Pieper stresses, "The whole span of creaturely existence between being and nothingness can never be understood, then, as though the relationship to nothingness were simply to be assigned equal rank with the relationship to being— or were even to be ranked before or above it. The 'way' of *homo viator* . . . leads toward being and away from nothingness; it leads to realization, not to annihilation. . . . "[25] If Pieper is correct, despair must always be seen as a dangerous temptation, never a true accounting of reality, more a demonic enchantment than stoic resignation to what is real. "Despair is self-contradictory, self-divisive," he explains. "In despair man actually denies his own desire, which is as indestructible as himself."[26]

Hope lives through magnanimity. The magnanimous person is the woman or man who strives after greatness, the person who both believes in and seeks what is most hopeful and promising for their lives. It is through magnanimity that we keep our eyes fixed on the great promises to which God has called us and refuse to be denied the most graced and glorious possibilities for our lives. Magnanimity is striving for excellence, especially the excellence that is the kingdom of God and fellowship with the saints. The magnanimous person refuses to be pusillanimous, refuses to be cowardly and meek about the hope-filled adventure to which God calls us in Christ, and refuses to allow anyone or any situation to steal his or her confidence about the blessed meaning and purpose of life.

Does magnanimity abound in our world today? Aren't there many people who don't hope for much of anything? Too many people who live for nothing more ennobling than seeking pleasures and satisfying their immediate needs? How often do we hear anyone describe life as a journey in hope, a pilgrimage to something immensely promising? In many ways the lack of hope we see around us may be connected with a loss of belief in something truly graced, blessed, and promising. Many people have slipped into the numbness of dejection and the frozen terror of despair because they no longer believe in the narratives of God's goodness and faithfulness as rehearsed for us in the story of Israel and the sending of Jesus. Many people do little more than live from day to day because they no longer believe there is a story worth living, a story truly worthy of the gift of our lives.

In contrast to magnanimity, more and more people today display all the symptoms of *acedia*. Acedia is a dangerous form of depression, a depression bordering on despair, and traditionally has been classified as one of the seven deadly sins because it is a condition of soul that brings death to one's spirit. What makes acedia dangerous is that like so many diseases of the spirit, we can be inflicted with it and not be aware of it. We can suffer from acedia and presume all is well, especially if we meet all the canons of success (wealth, possessions, pleasures, power, popularity, busyness) outlined by our culture.

Acedia describes a pervasive sadness and disillusionment that descends upon the person who no longer believes great things are possible in life. It is a deep listlessness of spirit, a life-robbing sadness, that characterizes the person who moves through life engaged by nothing hopeful or worthwhile. In *The Seven Deadly Sins Today*, Henry Fairlie describes acedia as "a morbid inertia"[27] that immobilizes a person. It is dejection in its most toxic form. What makes it morally and spiritually dangerous is that so many are barely aware of the malaise that cripples their lives because they have distracted themselves sufficiently to be oblivious to their own despair. They think that because they are busy, stimulated, active, and entertained that all is well.

But it isn't. Being entertained is not the same as living in hope. Staying distracted, whether it be by television, videos, the Internet, or shopping is usually more a strategy of desperation than a sign of deep contentment. Acedia is melancholy that can descend upon a person and remain with him so long that he hardly remembers the hope he has lost. Indeed, more often than not, he fears to remember and so becomes a master at living a distracted and inattentive life. Doesn't this describe many of us? Do we flood our lives with gadgets and trivialities only because we secretly fear the silence and simplicity that would reveal how empty and hopeless we have become?

The hope that has slipped away from us is the great hope God holds out for us in Christ, the hope that says we are destined not for nothingness and absurdity, not for the fleeting and superficial distractions with which we clutter our lives, but for fulsome participation in the peace, beatitude, and love of God. Pieper says acedia is a species of sadness that grows from a loss of belief in "the divine good" in us and represents a lack of courage "for the great things that are proper to the nature of the Christian."[28] Ultimately, the despair that flows from acedia is rooted in our rejection of the glory and nobility God has endowed us with as children of God. Indeed, acedia means "in the last analysis, that man will not be what God wants him to be—in other words, that he will not be what he really is."[29] In words that are disturbingly descriptive of our age, Pieper concludes, "Acedia is the signature of every age that seeks, in its despair, to shake off the obligations of that nobility of being that is conferred by Christianity and so, in its despair, to deny its true self."[30]

This is why the church is so important if there is to be a restoration of hope in our world. If it is true that acedia is a dominant characteristic of our times—and sometimes even of the church—then we need a people, a community, committed to embodying a genuine story of hope and of embracing possibilities that are graciously ennobling. We need a people who steadfastly witness that God's promises are real. If the Christian story is anything, it is a story of unabashed and jubilant hope because it tells us that a God who fashioned us from love and who lives with us in love will never abandon us. It tells us that a God who was generous enough to share life with us wants to give us everything God has: God's perfect happiness, God's perfect peace, God's everlasting joy. We who already are sharers in divinity are summoned to partake in God's life completely, and there is no more hopeful story than that.

But the story has to be heard, and it has to be seen. A people thirsty for hope but skeptical of its possibility need to see in their midst a people—an *ekklesia*—of hope. They need to see before them a community that is joyous because it has found hope and has found hope not because it is naive or *hopelessly* innocent but because it has heard good news, taken it to heart, and is living it joyfully. To go back to Hassler's novel, nobody should ever feel "north of hope" if the church is being faithful. The real "Hope Unit" should not be the psychiatric ward but the church, the body of Christ.

When he was writing about the virtue of hope, theologian Thomas Aquinas said hope is the virtue by which we believe something difficult is nonetheless possible to attain.[31] He added, "usually only with the help of others." We are "much more inclined to be hopeful," he said, "when we have friends to rely on."[32]

In his reflections on hope Aquinas was not only being theological, he was also being practical. His point is that hope is not a solitary virtue because we never hope *alone,* we always hope *together.* Hope is not something we can achieve for ourselves. Instead, it is a gift we receive, first from God in grace, Christ, and the Spirit, but also from those who stand by us and refuse to abandon us as we are challenged to fathom the darkness.

None of us can hope alone. We need companions in hope. This is why hope is connected to friendship and community and is impossible without them. Just as we are less likely to get lost on a trip when a friend accompanies us, so too none of us can make our way alone on the journey to God's kingdom without getting sidetracked, even lost. We are bound to lose our way in discouragement and disappointment if there are not others journeying with us who remind us where we are going and help us along the way. These companions in hope keep us from getting snared by desolation and dejection. They remind us that we need not and cannot sustain hope by ourselves because hope is a shared virtue; perhaps better, hope is a partnership Christians have with one another in Christ. This is why it is good for us to reflect on who have been our companions in hope.

But, like everything else in the Christian life, we are not to hoard this hope; we are to share it. Several years ago I heard a preacher tell a story, perhaps apocryphal, about the writer Robert Louis Stevenson, that offers a compelling metaphor for the power of a Christian's witness of hope.[33] According to the story, when Stevenson was a young boy growing up in Edinburgh, Scotland, he would often watch the village lamplighter making his rounds, lighting each of the street lamps one by one. Supposedly Stevenson once said, "Look, there is a man who punches holes in the darkness." That is what our companions in hope do for us and we do for them: we "punch holes in the darkness."

This is the hope the church should be bringing to the world. More than anyone, Christians should be people who "punch holes in the darkness." Instead of surrendering to the numbing despair that characterizes our age, we should rage against it by showing where real hope can be found. There is no more holy ministry we can offer our world today than to be a "Hope Unit," to be a church, a people, whose very way of life is an invitation to hope. If we do this, we can be sure, in the words of John Chrysostom, that we will "astound them by our way of life."

seven

Setting the World on Fire

Friendship with God and a Commitment to Justice

"I have come to light a fire on the earth. How I wish the blaze were ignited! I have a baptism to receive. What anguish I feel till it is over! Do you think I have come to establish peace on the earth? I assure you, the contrary is true; I have come for division. From now on, a household of five will be divided three against two and two against three; father will be split against son and son against father, mother against daughter and daughter against mother, mother-in-law against daughter-in-law, daughter-in-law against mother-in-law" (Luke 12:49–53).

Anytime this passage is read, preachers get nervous and congregations edgy because it is not a side of Jesus we like to see. We prefer the warm and reassuring Jesus, the Jesus who says he wants to unburden us and refresh our souls. We like the calm and consoling Jesus—the *befriending* Jesus—not the threatening Jesus who promises fire and division. But here Luke presents a Jesus who is not so embraceable, a Jesus we might flee rather than follow because he promises that anyone who takes up his message will be a cause of misunderstanding, discomfort, and possibly rejection.

Jesus comes not only to bless the world but also to change it. Jesus comes to work a transformation so searing it is like fire

139

burning away the old so that something unmistakably new can begin. In line with the prophets who preceded him, the fire is the fire of justice, the purifying, innovative, and re-creating justice of God that makes all things new. What is burnt away and left as ashes when the justice of God's reign appears is the demonic injustice that thwarts and frustrates life. It is an injustice that has held sway over the world for too long, and it is this injustice that Jesus, in inaugurating the reign of God, has come to dismantle. As Luke makes clear, this message will evoke derision from all who prosper from injustice and are threatened by the promise to rearrange the world according to the justice of God. Those who thrive on the misfortunes of others will crucify anyone who exposes their sin and pledges to overcome them. Such was the fate of Jesus, God's prophet of justice, and such is often the fate of those who risk the vocation of friendship with God and vow themselves to continuing the re-creation Jesus began.

Jesus says he has a "baptism to receive," and so do we. We who have been baptized in his name have been baptized into his life and ministry. To "put on Christ" is, as St. Paul reminds us, to put on "the mind of Christ." It is to commit ourselves to learning, embodying, and practicing the attitudes, concerns, and desires of Christ. Jesus had a passion for justice; his heart was ablaze with the desire to bring God's justice to the world, especially to the very ones crushed by the world's indifference. As God's prophet, Jesus knew God's dream for the world, a dream of the world not only redeemed and reconciled but also remade according to God's justice and love. Jesus called this re-creation of the world in justice the reign of God, and he commissioned his followers—the community of the friends of God—to carry on what he began by having the same passion for justice afire in their hearts.

The church is called to embody and work for the justice of God in the world. We are not to be a church of complacency and conformity, but a church that dares to be a source of division and misunderstanding for the sake of justice. We are adept at shirking this responsibility because there is always a cost to taking the reign of God seriously, especially when we see it not as a distant possibility but as a vision of how we are to live now. One of the most glaring ways we make Christianity safe and rob the gospel of its power is by muting the unmistakable call to jus-

tice that was central to the ministry of Jesus. We transform Jesus
from a prophet of justice proclaiming the kingdom of God to an
itinerant therapist who is little more than a chaplain for our
souls. Such a distortion not only seriously misreads the gospel
but also violates the message and mission of Jesus.

Like Jesus' contemporaries, a lot of us do not want to hear
about justice when we gather on Sundays for worship. We prefer friendlier, more upbeat messages about how Jesus likes us
and how we are pleasing to God. And we certainly do not want
to be told we cannot be good Christians unless we show in our
lives a commitment to justice and seek everyday the justice of
God. We squirm when priests and preachers speak about justice because it is like having ourselves exposed. Few of us feel
we are as concerned about justice as we ought to be, and most
of us, if we are honest, would prefer not being reminded of it. It
would be better, we think, if justice were a gospel option, a kind
of hood ornament to the Christian life but not quintessential to
that life. We would prefer it if a commitment to justice could be
left to the malcontents who are interested in changing the world,
instead of being told that we cannot be true disciples without
that commitment.

Any community who claims to be the friends of God has to
be on fire for the justice of God. Any community who claims to
know God must strive to live according to the justice of God.
There can be no true friendship with God apart from zeal for
the justice of God, no real relationship with God without a
corresponding commitment to work for the well-being of others, especially those whom injustice most often ravages. Friends
are people who see the same truth and who are committed to
the same goals and purposes. Therefore, anyone who claims
friendship with God risks embracing the mission and ministry
of God. As the Scriptures make clear, it is foremost a mission
and ministry of justice.

Justice: The Mission and Ministry of God

In *What Does the Lord Require? The Old Testament Call to
Social Witness*, Bruce C. Birch illustrates how from the very
beginning of salvation history, God's desire was that all creation

live in harmony and enjoy wholeness and well-being, a condition disclosed by the Hebrew *shalom*.[1] In the Book of Genesis the perfection of *shalom* is symbolized in the Garden of Eden, the paradisaical state where all creation thrives because everything lives in right relationship. Justice is the virtue of living in right relationship—a kind of friendship really—with God, with other human beings, and with the whole of nonhuman creation. In the Garden of Eden, God's "original justice"—creation blessed and flourishing *together*—is revealed. The God who blessed all of creation, declared every bit of it good, and is passionately concerned for its well-being is preeminently a God of justice, a God who orders the world so that all creatures may enjoy fully the life God desires for them.

Yahweh's passion for justice is further revealed in the deliverance of the Israelites from slavery in Egypt. God's call of Moses to be his instrument of deliverance and liberation indicates that Yahweh, God of the Israelites, may be Lord of all creation but is no remote, aloof Deity unmoved by the affliction of his people. The Old Testament, particularly the Book of Exodus, depicts God as both sovereign over creation and intimately connected to it; indeed, so intimately linked to the unfolding history of the world that God partakes in it and is eternally affected by it. God's compassion for Israel originates in God's deep involvement in the well-being of all he created, an involvement so complete that God enters into the suffering and brokenness of the world. In this respect, God's intimate participation in human history, especially the history of suffering, exquisitely demonstrates God's befriending love. As Birch comments, "For the Hebrews, to know meant a total involvement with and experiencing of that which is known. For God to *know* Israel's suffering is a revelation of unique involvement of the divine with the human condition. This is the beginning point of the Christian conception of a suffering God. God suffers as we suffer. God participates in our pain and brokenness."[2]

This may be the most decisive revelation about God in the Old Testament. The God who brings us to life through love never abandons us but continually befriends us by partaking intimately in every experience of our lives. God's love is the creative source of all that lives, the true original blessing; but in the unfolding history of creation, a history written more in tears and bloodshed than in harmony and peace, that divine love is most often expressed in solidarity and compassion for those who suffer, particularly when those sufferings are the harvest of injustice. From the call of Moses to the sometimes withering accusations of the prophets, Yahweh is revealed as God of the poor and oppressed, a God who befriends the downtrodden and destitute because so many times nobody else does. *God takes sides,* as the Scriptures make clear, and God always sides on behalf of the poor, the victimized ones who are forever deprived of the life and well-being that was God's desire for them from the beginning.

It is precisely the richness of God's compassion that explains the intensity of God's anger toward injustice. It is because *God knows the suffering of his people* that God grasps the crushing cruelty of injustice and responds not in acquiescence but with the promise of deliverance. The Exodus event is a defining moment in the history of Israel because it shatters all doubt about how God feels about injustice. God is never for injustice; God is always for life. God is never for oppression and poverty and homelessness and destitution; God is always for freedom and deliverance and hope. God's wrath is directed against the oppressors of the world, those Pharaohs, wherever and whenever they live, who thrive by crushing others and who build their power on the backs of the poor. In God, compassion and deliverance are inseparable because compassion is incomplete without a commitment to justice. Justice is compassion enacted.

Israel's deliverance from injustice and oppression into freedom and life was a paradigmatic event in its history—a story to be continually recalled as they remembered the good things God had done for them—because of what it taught them about God as well as themselves. God's intervention through Moses showed that even if love is the definitive attribute of God, God's love can never be separated from justice. Yahweh is a God of justice who seeks justice for all his creatures. Moreover, because God is revealed through justice, there can be no authentic knowledge of God apart from a commitment to justice. In the Bible, knowledge of God comes through the doing of justice; we know God when we live justly, we encounter God when we work on behalf of all the world's victims. As John Donahue writes, "The doing of justice is not the application of religious faith, but its sub-

stance; without it, God remains unknown."[3] This is why all talk
of living in friendship with God without a concomitant commitment to justice is nothing more than a beguiling deception.
Like the God whose mission they have made their own, the
friends of God must be practitioners of justice.

Thus, as the prophets eloquently testify (Amos 5:21–24; Isa.
1:10–17; Micah 6:6–7), all the liturgies and worship in the world
are worthless in bringing knowledge of God and empty of praise
to God if injustice rules our hearts and prospers in our world.
God may want to be glorified, but God is most eminently glorified not through feasts and gaudy liturgical celebrations but
through practices of justice. In the Bible, the test of true religion is not measured in our adherence to liturgical rubrics but
in our becoming a just people, a community passionate about
justice not as an alternative to true worship but as both a pre-
condition for it and an expression of it. Without justice, we can
chant and sing all we want and bathe ourselves in incense, but
we will remain ignorant of the God we claim to praise, and the
emptiness of our prayers will reflect the depth of our delusion.
Apart from a commitment to justice, our friendship with God
is sheer pretense and our promises of faithfulness lies.

In the Bible, salvation may be intensely personal, but it is also
inescapably social. If sin describes "how *shalom*, wholeness, gets
broken,"[4] whether we are talking about the brokenness of our
lives or the brokenness of our world, then it is through God's
gift of salvation, a salvation that culminates in perfect justice
for all God's creatures, that it is restored. If justice both creates
and sustains a right relationship, injustice breeds disharmony
by twisting and disordering our relationships—relationships
defined more by brokenness and annihilation than well-being
and life. This is why God's salvation can never be a purely personal deliverance. Salvation is inherently social and political
because it involves God's act of overcoming the ravages of injustice in order to restore the blessings of life. As John Haughey
writes, "Yahweh prepared Israel over the course of the centuries
to expect a salvation which was social in its form with justice as
its content."[5]

The Exodus event not only taught the Israelites important lessons about God and how God's spirit works in history, it likewise told them the kind of people they were called to be and how

God expected them to live. True, they were a people set free from slavery by God, but they were set free for a purpose. They were specially chosen by God and lived in a covenant relationship with God, but with the grace of their call came an urgent responsibility. They were to witness to God's ways and work for God's plans in history, and the memory of their own deliverance told them the freedom, justice, and life God desired for them was equally God's intention for all peoples. As God's covenant people, the Israelites were entrusted with a mission, the mission of embodying and enacting God's justice for the world. Like the church—the community of the friends of God today—they were to be God's "instrument of grace in this sinful and broken world,"[6] remembering that God's grace always works to overcome injustice and reestablish *shalom.*

In this respect, Israel's call to be a people of justice was rooted in a gift. For them to seek justice for others was to live in grateful remembrance of the gift they had received. Israel's commitment to justice was both an expression of gratitude and nurtured by gratitude, gratitude to God for their deliverance from servitude in Egypt. Like anyone who has received grace, they had to ask how they were to respond to that grace. What they discovered is that the grace that gave them freedom and life also gave them a communal identity and a special responsibility. As God's covenant people, they were to live according to the grace they had received by seeking justice and liberation for others. "At Sinai, Israel became God's people, called upon to embody the experience of God's deliverance in a community for whom love of God was intimately bound with love of neighbor (Lev. 19:18)," Birch writes. "Israel was liberated *from* oppression and suffering but was liberated *for* community and mutual responsibility."[7] Put differently, they were to *befriend* the poor and needy in their midst with the same liberating justice with which God had befriended them.

What we learn from the story of Israel is that justice is both a gift and a responsibility, both a grace and a call. Israel was freed from injustice not only that they might be delivered from oppression but also that they might be the community of God's compassionate justice in the world. They had experienced God's gracious deliverance, but they were to extend that blessing to others by being agents of justice themselves, especially in the active concern they showed the most forgotten and neglected persons around them. If they truly understood the grace they had received, they would embody God's compassionate justice not only in their relationship with other members of the covenant community but also with every neighbor who came their way.

The Exodus experience called Israel to be a particular kind of community with a distinctive way of life. They were to pattern their life on the liberating justice of God and be a people who showed the same compassionate care for the poor and oppressed as God had shown to them. They were to be an agent of God's purposes in the world by faithfully carrying out the mission of liberating justice God had entrusted to them. If God's dream for the world, indeed for the whole of creation, is a world characterized by justice, harmony, and peace, then Israel, God's covenant community, was to allow this dream to be fulfilled through them. Similarly, if God's dream of restoration and renewal for all creatures is to be realized today, God needs a faithful people, a community passionate for justice, committed to making that dream happen. In the Old Testament this commitment to justice was integral to the vocation of the chosen people, and today it is a central dimension of the vocation of the church.

What practically does this mean? For Israel it meant they were not to be "like the nations" whose social and economic order reflected a politics of domination; rather, as people faithful to the compassionate justice of God, they were to be an alternative community whose social, economic, and political order was determined not by the patterns of Egypt or Mesopotamia but by the characteristics of their God.[8] As people of the covenant, Israel's social and economic structures and activities were to be shaped by a "daring vision," a vision of "radical societal renewal"[9] in which the dignity and well-being of every member was safeguarded. It was a vision of profound social and economic transformation away from patterns of oppression and inequity in which large groups of people were permanently locked out of society toward patterns of inclusion, participation, and equality.

Specifically, fidelity to the covenant demanded that in their lives together and in their dealings with others they practice a "politics of justice," not domination and exclusion, and an "economics of equality."[10] A politics of justice entails a strong affirmation of the dignity, worth, and equality of all persons before God and a social order that both reflects and respects that affirmation. As the opposite of a politics of elitism and exclusion that structures society to insure the enhancement of a few over the diminishment of the many, a politics of justice and inclusion asserts that no one is expendable because everyone matters.

Similarly, an economics of equality describes an economic order characterized by equitable access to the goods, opportunities, and resources of society and an equitable distribution of the goods and resources of society.[11] The primary aim of an economics of equality is to ensure that the basic needs of all persons are met and never is there a time when an excess of wealth and material goods for one person or group means a lack of necessary resources for others. Thus, Israel was to construct a social and economic order in which the well-being of no one was ever forgotten. No one lived in need, no one was marginalized or powerless, and no one was ever oppressed. In short, a politics of justice and an economics of equality were not a utopian dream; they were God's will, and if Israel was faithful to God's will and the demands of the covenant, "there would be no poverty and need"[12] among them.

Justice in the Mission and Ministry of Jesus

If the Old Testament presents Yahweh as a God of justice, a God whose intention at the beginning of creation is to order all things in right relationship and to ensure the well-being of all creation, both human and nonhuman, how is the divine passion for justice extended into the mission and ministry of Jesus? In his inaugural homily in the synagogue at Nazareth, Jesus announces the purpose of his mission. He has been anointed by God "to bring glad tidings to the poor, to proclaim liberty to captives, recovery of sight to the blind and release to prisoners, to announce a year of favor from the Lord" (Luke 4:18–19). Jesus not only identifies himself with God's mission and ministry of justice but in his proclamation of the coming of the reign of God makes it clear that God's kingdom, which has entered the world in him, is supremely a kingdom of justice, and this kingdom is meant to renew and re-create the world. In Jesus we see that the reign of God is the justice of God, and the justice of God is "the power of God active in the world, transforming it and confronting the powers of the world"[13] that so often are powers of injustice and oppression.

The life and ministry of Jesus testify that his mission is to bring God's justice and peace to all people, especially the victims of the world. Jesus never understands the kingdom of God to refer simply to a paradisaical future; quite the contrary, the kingdom of God represents how the world is to be remade now according to the justice of God. For Jesus, the kingdom of God is inherently political because of its repercussions on the social and economic order of our world.

Jesus' commitment to proclaiming, instituting, and embodying the reign of God demonstrates emphatically that Jesus never accepted injustice. In his reaching out to the poor and oppressed members of society, in his embrace of all the excluded ones, Jesus manifested his fierce opposition to all the powers of the world that crush and twist and annihilate. Jesus never accepted all the violence and oppression and grief spawned by injustice because they are not of God, but of the Evil One. Oppression, exclusion, destitution, and violence, all these are part of the dominion of death Jesus came not to endorse but to conquer.

Like Jesus, we who today vow to live in friendship with God should never resign ourselves to the demonic energies of injustice and exclusion as if they are sadly inevitable in a fallen and less than perfect world; rather, like Jesus, we should recognize these powers for what they are, all elements of the sovereignty of death that Jesus' death and resurrection have overcome. A temptation for all of us is complacency before the injustice of the world, especially if we are not immediately affected by it. But to surrender to injustice as a tragic necessity belies a lack of faith in the power of Jesus' resurrection and a failure of discipleship. Like Israel before us, Christians are to embrace God's vision for the world, a vision of *shalom* that seeks well-being and peace for all creatures, and steadfastly denounce and work to overcome all the energies of death.

Like Israel before us, Christians commit themselves to proclaiming and embodying the justice of God because, through

Jesus' passion, death, and resurrection, we have known our own exodus from the hopeless slavery to sin into the freedom that comes from Christ. We find this theme emphasized particularly in the writings of Paul. Paul stresses that the cross and resurrection of Jesus reversed our fate from being a people held captive in sin to a people who have been freed for the new life of grace. We have been "justified" through the "injustice" suffered by Jesus, the only truly innocent one, and hence are able now to live in a right relationship with God, all our neighbors, and even ourselves.[14]

Therefore, like the Israelites who remembered God's mercy to them, an essential element to a life of friendship with God is to remember God's gracious mercy toward us and to allow the power of that memory to impel us in being instruments of God's justice and mercy in the world. No true friend of God should ever have to ask why we should bother about justice. Any Christian with a glimmer of gratitude will commit to justice because she remembers God's goodness to us. For Christians, a commitment to justice is nothing more than gratitude to God for having justified us, setting us free in Christ. Gratitude comes from remembering well (ingratitude from remembering poorly), and Christians, particularly at worship, continually recall God's liberating grace in our lives so we may be agents of God's liberation and justice—emissaries of God's friendship—wherever it is needed in our world. This memory of our own deliverance ought never be a faint echo, much less sheer nostalgic recollection; rather, it should guide, shape, and direct our lives now so that we strive to extend to others the same justice, goodness, mercy, and life God has given us. As Paul testified, "For our sake God made Jesus to be sin who knew no sin, so that in him we might become the justice of God" (2 Cor. 5:21).

We are justified for the sake of justice, freed for the sake of freeing others. In Christ, John Haughey says, we are justified by God so we can *do* justice in the world. "The person is brought into the new creation and into the dynamism of the justice of God," he writes, "in order that justice might also be done through him and through the body of Christ of which he has been made a member."[15] What God has done for us we should strive to do for others, and thanks to the power of God's grace, we can. No Christian should ever underestimate his or her potential for trans-

formative action, because in Christ we are empowered to be
agents, even cocreators, in God's ongoing renewal of the world.
Our actions flow from and participate in the activity of God's
remaking of all things. This is why there is no excuse for surrender, no justification for defeat before the powers of injustice.

Friendship with God and the Practice of Justice

What does all of this mean for how Christians, the community of the friends of God, understand the nature and mission
of the church and, indeed, the Christian life? First, it should be
clear, as the bishops of the Roman Catholic church stated in
their 1971 document *Justice in the World*, that "Action on behalf
of justice and participation in the transformation of the world
fully appear . . . as a constitutive dimension of the preaching of
the Gospel, or, in other words, of the Church's mission for the
redemption of the human race and its liberation from every
oppressive situation."[16] A commitment to justice and action on
behalf of justice are not gospel options. The biblical witness
abundantly demonstrates that there is no authentic imitation of
Christ without a passionate, ongoing commitment to justice not
only in the most immediate relationships of our everyday lives
but also towards those who suffer from injustice anywhere in
our world. We cannot call ourselves true friends of God without working to reform any institutions (including our churches),
structures, and practices that perpetuate injustice. A commitment to justice has to be one of the identifying marks of the
church, a characteristic that helps us discriminate between true
Christian communities and false ones, between mimicking
friendship with God and truly embodying it.

It is important to stress this because in our society today, with
its emphasis on individualism, convenience, and pleasure, a
commitment to justice can seem nothing more than a lifestyle
choice, not a gospel necessity. We think that as long as somebody somewhere is working for justice, we do not need to be,
but this very privatized and selective interpretation of Christianity egregiously perverts the message and ministry of Jesus,
as well as the entire salvific activity of God. We cannot live in
friendship with God unless we look out for the well-being of oth-

ers, simply because friendship with God commits us to the plans and purposes of God.

Second, these reflections on the centrality of justice in salvation history indicate, theologian John Coleman says, that without a commitment to justice, "the Christian proclamation of redemption in Christ from structures of sin and death rings hollow."[17] Why should the victims of the world listen to our proclamation of the gospel, much less find hope in it, if we preach a message of liberation but do nothing to help them experience it in their lives? The church rightly loses credibility when it preaches about a justice it does nothing to achieve; such cowardice and hypocrisy suggest that the church itself is living unjustly or fears the risk any commitment to justice entails.

Evangelization must be accompanied by action on behalf of justice if it is to be more than empty words and hollow promises. The community of the friends of God deceives itself if it thinks it is honoring its vocation by proclaiming the gospel but doing nothing to unleash its transformative power in the world. If this is the case, the very idea of friendship with God becomes little more than pious self-absorption and bourgeois sentimentality, and not a summons to share in God's liberating re-creation of all things in justice and love. When the poor hear the gospel preached to them, they should see its message of justice, liberation, and peace fulfilled in their lives. Then they will know that the invitation to live in friendship with God does not signal a retreat from the sorrows and sufferings of the world but a call to participate in the most costly and hopeful adventure possible—the adventure of cooperating with God in exposing and overcoming injustice wherever it exists.

Third, God's passion for justice and concern for the poor calls the church to a prophetic role in society. This means first that the church has a responsibility to denounce (never accept) and work to overcome (never embrace) unjust institutions, structures, policies, and practices wherever they exist; this includes, of course, any injustice in our churches. Like the prophets of the Old Testament, the friends of God are called to speak the uncomfortable truths few want to hear about the sin of injustice, about how the complacency and indifference of some can mean destitution and death for many, and about how those who prosper through injustice are strangers to God and have no place in his kingdom.

This is a costly, even dangerous, commission because we live in a world that often prefers to repress the truth rather than be judged by it. Injustice thrives on the power of the lie, but the spirit of God is always a spirit of courageous truthfulness (John 16:13). A life of friendship with God should nurture in us the courage and skills necessary for speaking the truth—even unpleasant truths—not only to one another but also to our world. In societies—and sometimes, tragically, even in churches— structured on patterns of deceit more than truthfulness, such a commitment to the truth will be inescapably risky, but boldness about the truth is one way of distinguishing the true friend of God from the impostor. The capacity to speak and live the truth should be engendered in a life of friendship with God not only through the liturgy and worship of the church but also through lives of prayer, through the reception of the sacraments, through constant meditation on the Scriptures, and through ongoing communal support.

Moreover, the prophetic role of the church demands that the church live now, as best as it can, according to the kingdom justice it proclaims. No prophet has credibility if she is not a living symbol of what she calls others to be, and the same is true with the church. The prophetic message of the church is hollow and hypocritical if the church does not embody in its way of life, in its own structures, rules, principles, and practices, the justice of God to which it calls the world. At the very least, this would mean there should be no practices of exclusion in the church. It would mean the church should be one place where the dignity and equality of all persons in God is steadfastly affirmed. It should also mean that people find in the church patience, mercy, and compassion rather than harshness.

Justice, Friendship, and Solidarity

Justice is the virtue of community, the virtue that makes life together possible, whether that be in our families, in our churches, at the workplace, in our relationships with friends or strangers, in how one country treats another, or in how we relate to the natural world. Justice makes community possible by working to ensure right relationships on all levels of life; it is rooted in the vision of all human beings, indeed the whole of creation, bonded together in God. The aim of justice, then, is not only to help us recognize and appreciate these bonds of relationship but also to teach us how to live in a way that respects and strengthens them instead of ignoring, denying, or destroying them.

Where do we learn this? Obviously, the family is an important setting for learning how to share, how to attend to the needs and well-being of others, and how to work together for commonly shared goals. So is friendship. As we discussed in chapter 3, friendships are morally important because in them we learn how to honor consistently the claims another person has on us. If the heart of justice consists in respecting the dignity of persons and giving them their due, these are precisely the dispositions and skills that are honed in us through friendships. Thomas Aquinas defined justice as "the constant and steadfast willingness to give to each person what is his or hers by right,"[18] an essential moral skill learned through the practices of friendship. It is by learning how to seek the good of another in friendship that we gradually acquire the skill to act rightly toward every person with whom we come into contact, respecting their dignity, acknowledging their rights, and fulfilling our responsibilities towards them.

This may sound easy until we think about what it means to give every person who comes our way what is his or hers by right. The virtue of justice is relevant in every situation and circumstance of life, but the precise form justice should take depends on the nature of our relationship with another. This is why enacting the virtue of justice in the various relationships of our lives requires discriminating judgment and much discernment. For instance, what justice obliges friends to do for each other is in some respects different from what teachers owe students, doctors their patients, or pastors their congregations. Obviously, we owe our friends an availability, presence, loyalty, and attentiveness that teachers do not owe students, doctors their patients, or pastors their congregations. The responsibilities of justice differ. The virtue of justice disposes us to recognize that we owe all persons something, but that justice obliges us differently according to the various types of relationships is what friendship (and other special relationships) should teach us.

Justice should always be at the forefront of our consciousness because it is the fulcrum of every other moral obligation we have. Parents realize this quickly when they struggle with treating their children in a way that acknowledges both their equality and their distinctiveness. Teachers wrestle with justice when they ponder how to be fair to all their students while still taking individual circumstances into account. We feel the pinch of justice when we ponder how to negotiate the requests of a variety of friends. How can we treat all of our friends justly? How can we attend to the good of one without neglecting the well-being of the others? The challenge to discern exactly what justice requires in the diverse relationships and circumstances of our lives is what makes it such an essential but difficult moral skill to acquire. The person of justice is *habitually* disposed to take the needs and well-being of others into account. He recognizes the claim other people have on him and how he is responsible for them. Most of all, he has the wisdom to know how he is called to act justly towards them and what this practically would mean. Such a precious and indispensable skill should be cultivated in the crucible of friendship.

We cannot become persons of justice apart from a vision of solidarity, a vision that appreciates how we live in relationship with all human beings (and, indeed, the whole of creation). This, too, should be nurtured in friendship because, despite the preferential nature of every friendship, good friendships should always deepen our awareness of and sensitivity toward others. Friendships should enlarge our moral vision, never restrict it. Friendships should expand our compassion for others, not calcify it. As a mark of authentic friendship, a vision of solidarity sees the bonds we share with all of life. All people are part of us and we are part of them. We live in them and they in us because we all share the same source of life in God. As the Catholic activist and writer Dorothy Day frequently said, "We are all members one of another." Indeed, the bedrock fact about us is not our individuality but our solidarity.

It may be easy to grasp the importance of solidarity intellectually, but it is notoriously difficult to practice solidarity in our everyday lives. This is true not only because of our uncanny tendency to put ourselves first but also because of the individualism of our culture. In the United States today, solidarity is countercultural. We do not live in a culture that encourages us to see our connectedness to other human beings and our responsibilities toward them. We talk a lot about rights, but not so much about obligations to others. We emphasize our freedom of choice and our almost absolute right to pursue our own interests and to fulfill our own needs, but seldom do we speak of the common good and how our freedom might be used to serve the needs of others.

In his 1961 letter on social justice, "Christianity and Social Progress" (*Mater et Magistra*), Pope John XXIII wrote that we are "all members of one and the same household."[19] John used this image to appeal to our moral imaginations. If everyday I live thinking of every human being as a "member of one and the same household," it will change the way I see, think about, and act toward others. If someone is a member of my household, that means he is a member of my family, and if we are family members, we are intimately connected to one another and responsible for one another. If someone is a member of my family, I cannot be indifferent to him. As a member of my family, he has a claim on me and I have a responsibility toward him.

In his epic novel *The Grapes of Wrath*, John Steinbeck makes the same point. Through the musings of the fallen and reluctant preacher, Rev. Jim Casey, Steinbeck argues that the basic truth about humanity is that we are all one, and trouble starts when we forget this. Steinbeck suggests injustice happens anytime we deny our solidarity with others; all it takes is one unjust person—one person living out of solidarity—to mess things up. There is a scene in the novel where Casey reminisces about the time he, like Jesus, went into the wilderness. Alone at night, looking up at the stars, he has an insight that changes his life:

> "I ain't sayin' I'm like Jesus," the preacher went on. "But I got tired like Him, an' I got mixed up like Him, an' I went into the wilderness like Him, without no campin' stuff. Nighttime I'd lay on my back an' look up at the stars; morning I'd set an' watch the sun come up; midday I'd look out from a hill at the rollin' dry country; evenin' I'd foller the sun down. Sometimes I'd pray like I always done. On'y I couldn' figure what I was prayin' to or for.

There was the hills, an' there was me, an' we wasn't separate no
more. We was one thing. An' that one thing was holy."

"Hallelujah," said Granma, and she rocked a little, back and
forth, trying to catch hold of an ecstasy.

"An' I got thinkin', on'y it wasn't thinkin', it was deeper down
than thinkin'. I got thinkin' how we was holy when we was one
thing, an' mankin' was holy when it was one thing. An' it on'y got
unholy when one mis'able little fella got the bit in his teeth an'
run off his own way, kickin' an' draggin' an' fightin'. Fella like
that bust the holiness. But when they're all workin' together, not
one fella for another fella, but one fella kind of harnessed to the
whole shebang—that's right, that's holy."[20]

Justice and the Moral Imagination: Why How We Worship Matters

If injustice "busts the holiness," how do we cultivate a moral
imagination informed by solidarity? How do we, both as individuals and as a community, nurture the moral vision that makes
it possible for us to be agents of God's justice in the world? We
cannot presume that sustaining a vision of solidarity will be easy,
because there is much in ourselves and in our culture that erodes
it. The Christian community, the church, must be quite inten-
tional in fostering a moral and spiritual imagination informed
by solidarity.

How does this occur? In earlier chapters we discussed the
pivotal role of liturgy and worship in the church's moral formation. It is no different for sustaining a vision of solidarity and
for vivifying our commitment to justice. David Hollenbach
writes, "The moral imagination of Christians is shaped by all
the fundamental symbols and doctrines of the Christian faith.
The dimensions of this living imagination are most concretely
shaped and revealed in those moments where the symbolic
enactment of Christian belief is at its most intense—in the sacraments that are at the very heart of the church's life as a wor-
shipping community."[21]

Nowhere should the moral imagination of the church be nurtured more than in liturgy and worship. Worship ought to be
transformative for how we see and act; no one should enter into

the prayer of the church and walk away unchanged, even unshaken. What makes worship fearfully subversive in a world at home with injustice is that it should form a community that is not only scandalized by the plaintive litany of all the world's victims but is also equally committed to standing with them and working on their behalf. Any worship that does not fire our imaginations with God's vision of justice for the whole of creation is a sham, a shameful affront to the God in whose ways we claim to be walking.

The worship and liturgy of the church should deepen our concern for others and help us see our responsibilities toward them. It should remind us, the friends of God, of the connections we have with all people and cultivate in us a deep sensitivity for the needs of others. If this isn't happening, what do we mean when we say "Amen"? Isn't our "Amen" our assent to the story of God we want to continue? Isn't our "Amen" an emphatic yes to God's vision of justice and *shalom* for all creation? In her essay "Liturgy and Justice: An Intrinsic Relationship," Kathleen Hughes captures well how worship should transform us into a people of justice who commit ourselves to being agents of God's care in the world. She writes,

> With every Amen we join ourselves to the paschal mystery and pledge ourselves to that vision of justice and love that is inherent in the celebration. Amen is an act of faith and an act of commitment. Full, conscious, and active participation in the celebration of the liturgy demands that we will, *in deed*, live what we proclaim.[22]

Worship, particularly the Eucharist, ought to be a sign of solidarity and unity not only among Christians but also with all of humanity. If, through the death and resurrection of Jesus, God overcomes the brokenness and divisions of life and reconciles all of us to God and one another, then nowhere more than at worship should we learn to reimagine the world according to the compassionate justice of God. How can we, the friends of God, abide the brokenness of the world if we understand what God has done for us? Remembering the reconciliation and unity that comes to us in Christ should animate us to work for the same healing and restoration in our world.

But perhaps more than anything, the Eucharist should fire our imaginations with a vision of solidarity and justice simply because the Eucharist is all about being fed. As Hollenbach notes, "the shared meal is the preeminent symbol of God's will for the human race."[23] The Eucharist shows us that God's desires are concrete and practical and urgent: God wants people to be fed, clothed, sheltered, and cared for. In the Eucharist we are fed so that we might feed others. In the Eucharist we are nurtured and cared for by God so that we might show to others, especially the least fortunate, the love and care God has extended to us. The Eucharist testifies that justice is not an abstraction; rather, justice is enfleshed in the most concrete and necessary of human activities, the activity of eating and being fed.

But do not forget that those who gather around a table at the Eucharist are not an assortment of strangers but a people who have become a community—a covenant people—thanks to God's merciful rescue. As we feast on the body and blood of Christ, our eyes should be opened to see that our solidarity extends far beyond those who might be gathered with us in worship. The Christ who comes to us in the Eucharist is the same Christ who challenges us to see him in all members of the family of God, especially those excluded and forgotten ones we are most accustomed not to see at all (Matt. 25:31–46). This is the vision that fires the moral imagination of the friends of God, and one they should joyfully strive to practice.

If, as we saw in chapter 1, the church is summoned to move from "the destructively familiar to the creatively strange," there is nothing more destructively familiar than the injustice, destitution, and oppression that continue to crucify our world, and nothing more creatively and hopefully strange than the promise of justice restored and *shalom* reestablished through God's reign. But the reign of God is both a future promise and an already established reality. The kingdom of God broke into our world in Jesus and should continue to live through the church. Justice beats at the heart of the reign of God, and there is nothing more stunning the friends of God can do for the world than to "light a fire on the earth" by living the justice of God. It is one dream we should never allow to die.

eight

Not Letting Hurt Have the Final Word

Friendship and the Practice of Forgiveness

Here's a story about forgiveness. The Mountain Laurel Festival is a springtime pageant held every year in Pineville, a little town nestled in the mountains of southeastern Kentucky. In 1971, my sister Mary was a senior at Spalding College in Louisville and had been chosen to represent her school at the Mountain Laurel Festival.

Mary was thrilled, but she also needed an escort, and since all this happened at the last minute, she knew it might not be easy to find someone to accompany her to Pineville. She did what all sisters would do: she asked me, her brother. I had no desire to spend a weekend in Pineville, and no desire to go to the Mountain Laurel Festival. Having recently turned twenty, I figured I had better things to do than to escort my sister to a weekend pageant in the mountains, so I came up with a lot of lame excuses. I told Mary I was too busy. I told her I was sure she could find someone else to take her, although I knew that at the last minute this might not be easy. In my conscience I knew what I ought to do. I knew I should say yes. I knew this weekend meant a lot to her, and I knew it was no great incon-

159

venience to me to go with her. But I still said no. I knew I was
being stubbornly selfish and that my refusal would hurt my sister, but I wouldn't budge.

The story has a happy ending for two reasons. First, Mary did
find an escort, and the weekend at the Mountain Laurel Festival went well.

Second, Mary forgave me. Not right away, but she did forgive me. My sister was not happy when I said no. My inability
to do what brothers ought to do hurt her very much. She was
rightly angry and disappointed; however, eventually she was
able to reach beyond that anger, hurt, and disappointment and
forgive me.

It is funny what we remember. There are some memories we
hold onto for life, and this is one of them for me. I never want
to forget what happened in the spring of 1971—not because I
enjoy reminiscing about my failures, but because it taught me
the absolute importance of forgiveness and the need to move to
reconciliation if we are not to be controlled by the failures, mistakes, hurts, and disappointments of our lives. I learned how
crucial it is that we be able to forgive others and allow ourselves
to be forgiven by them. I learned how indispensable forgiveness
is to any human life if we are not to be prisoners of the hurts
and failures of our past.

Life together is impossible without the power of forgiveness.
Everyone knows this, but friends may know it better than most.
No matter how hard we try to live at peace with one another—
even with the best friends of our lives—eventually something
comes between us: hurts and disappointments, infidelities, broken relationships and broken hearts, terrible mistakes, malicious remarks, unintended slights, or promises betrayed. It happens all the time, even among the closest of friends. We hurt and
we get hurt. We disappoint and we are disappointed. Every intimate friendship has occasionally run aground on the shoals of
pettiness, thoughtlessness, and even maliciousness. We either
deal with these things through forgiveness and reconciliation
or the friendship ends and our lives are easily ruled by anger,
bitterness, and resentment.

We have to be able to move on, but we cannot move on in life
together unless we are willing to forgive and be forgiven. Without the gift of forgiveness, no friendship could endure. For-

giveness is the love that holds life together, the love that enables us to go on as friends, as spouses, as family members or colleagues, in hope. Life is a matter of going on together, not only because God calls us to communion and peace with one another but also because we need one another and depend on one another. Our lives are enriched by others, especially by our friends. This is why every relationship that is lost to something unforgiven impoverishes us.

All of us know this. We know that if we are not able to forgive or to be forgiven, something much more important is lost. Without forgiveness we cut ourselves off from life and grow alienated not only from our friends, the very people we once considered the greatest gifts of our lives, but also from God, and even from ourselves; without forgiveness we place ourselves in exile. Forgiveness is the love that always gives new life. It is the love that frees us from a painful past so we can know a hopeful future.

Nobody should appreciate the importance of forgiveness more than Christians should. We are able to live in friendship with God only because we have first been forgiven by God. We live *from* the gift of forgiveness; indeed, we have life at all only because of the undeserved extravagant mercy of an always befriending God. Perhaps more than anyone, Christians should be practiced in the art of forgiveness because Christianity itself is the call to live a forgiven and forgiving life. We who have been shown mercy must extend it to others. We who have been reconciled to God and to one another through the cross of Christ must never allow hurt and brokenness to prevail. Indeed, forgiveness lies at the heart of a life of friendship with God, and is one of the most timely gifts the church—the community of the friends of God—can witness to the world.

Cultivating a Forgiven and Forgiving Heart

When I was young, we used to go each summer to an amusement park in the west end of Louisville called Fontaine Ferry Park. One of the rides was the bumper cars. The whole point of the bumper cars was to crash into somebody. Even if you tried, it was impossible to avoid collisions because the slippery, greased surface guaranteed everyone was bumping into somebody.

Sometimes life is like the bumper cars. No matter how hard we try to live well with others or how good and just we try to be, inevitably we hurt one another and disappoint one another, and sometimes we do this most to the people we love. Like the bumper cars, everyday life can seem geared for collisions. Even the best friendships tumble when we bruise each other through little insensitivities, when we fall short of the love we've promised to give, when we succumb to small acts of malice, or when we become better at withdrawing into ourselves than giving of ourselves. So many of our recollections are regrets about things we wish we had never done but now cannot erase. This is why in our everyday life together, including our friendships, we need to grow in the art of forgiveness. We need to be skilled in the virtue that enables us to deal with all the setbacks and tensions of ordinary life, most of them minor but some, unfortunately, that are monumental.

How could we live together at all if we were not able to forgive and be forgiven? All the pivotal relationships of our lives could have broken down forever if we were not able to reach out to one another in forgiveness. Every marriage, every friendship, any communal life together, when we look at any of these, we know there are points when we could easily say, "It could have ended here." We need the life-giving love of forgiveness because it is the only power we have against the bumps and bruises of life. Sometimes the slights we suffer or inflict are trifling; other times they scar us or others for life. No matter how deep the hurts and disappointments may reach, we have to be able to start over, to pick up the pieces and begin again in hope.

I sometimes wonder what would have happened if my sister had closed her heart and refused me forgiveness. What would have happened if Mary had taken that justified hurt and anger and chosen to nurse them instead of overcoming them through forgiveness? It would have spelled a loss of freedom for both of us: for me, because it would have been much more difficult to move beyond the guilt and regret that held me captive; for Mary, because she would have lost her freedom to a hurt that would only grow deeper. No matter how understandable her hurt, if Mary had chosen to nurse resentment instead of forgiveness, she would have been prisoner to a hurt that would never be healed.

No matter how hard it can be to forgive, what is the alternative to forgiveness? As difficult and preposterous and unfair as forgiveness sometimes seems, is there a better way to go about life?

Judy Logue explores this in *Forgiving the People You Love to Hate.* She says if we have been hurt and harmed by others, we must "face the enemies of our hearts,"[1] those wounds, hurts, and resentments that can imprison us in bitterness if we do not open them to forgiveness. Unhealed, the hurts and resentments harden. Untouched by the grace of forgiveness, they grow stronger and start to master our lives, so that in ways we hardly suspect, we lose freedom and joy to them. At that point, Logue observes, "It is not so much that we have resentments but rather that resentments have us."[2] Like the deep-sea diver who plumbs the depths of the ocean, we must go down into the depths of our hearts and scrutinize those regions of hurt, bitterness, and resentment in order to see what might need the healing power of forgiveness. We must ask questions such as, What hurt is keeping me from being free? or What disappointment do I keep revisiting? Or, as Logue puts it, "Who do we love to hate?"

It is no secret that sometimes we do not want to be freed from the hurts and disappointments of life because we have almost come to enjoy them. We might not like what we suffered, but we can, oddly enough, like returning to the hurt and nurturing it. If nothing else, keeping the hurt alive gives us a little power over those who hurt us. We may have our wounds, but if we keep them visible and fresh, they are a constant reminder to the one who hurt us that the hurt is still there.

If we are honest, we know that holding on to a hurt is much easier than growing beyond it. The hurts and disappointments of our lives can give us a ready excuse not to be responsible. Instead of moving forward, we settle into those hurts and let them define our lives. We have all known people who have made hurts their home. They have grown so comfortable with their resentments that they find them a cozy place in which to live. As Logue says, "Sometimes the resentment toward the offender is so old and so familiar that we cannot imagine life without it; we've almost come to find it entertaining. In truth, it is scary to let go of something we have nurtured with all our hearts for a very long time."[3]

Perhaps we have sometimes behaved this way with our friends. We can nurture "with all our hearts" not the liberating grace of forgiveness, which would renew and strengthen the friendship, but the hard brittleness of hate. We can choose to give our hearts not to the healing of reconciliation but to the stony coldness of bitterness. We can settle not into the grace of forgiveness but into the hurts and hatreds of our lives until they become so comfortable and familiar that we cannot imagine ourselves without them. We can enjoy telling the same old stories of betrayal and disappointment over and over again as we continually remind our friends of how they let us down and then wonder why those friendships die.

Forgiveness makes change possible, but only if we really want to change. Forgiveness carries the promise of healing and new life for friendships damaged by thoughtlessness or neglect, but not if we prefer to play it safe with resentment. Forgiveness can free us from the wounds, hurts, and brokenness that are so debilitating for friendships, but only if we are willing to move beyond them by offering to our friends the forgiveness we ourselves so often need. Forgiveness can always work, but a large part of the responsibility for forgiveness lies not on the shoulders of the friends we sometimes need to forgive but with us who need to offer it. As comforting as it can sometimes be to harbor hurts instead of moving beyond them, to do so is to make a decision to die by closing ourselves to grace. That is always a temptation, but it is one sin against the Spirit we can never survive.

This is why Jesus prods and pushes us to forgive. We see this in one of the most memorable stories of forgiveness in the New Testament. It's in the gospel of Matthew, chapter 18, and, not surprisingly, Peter is involved. Peter approaches Jesus to ask how many times he has to forgive. We do not know the background of the story, but we do know Peter never asks such questions merely out of intellectual curiosity. Maybe Peter has been hurt to such an extent that he begins to wonder if he can shut certain people out of his life. Maybe there is someone Peter has regularly had to forgive, but instead of amending his life on account of being forgiven, the ungrateful fellow uses it as an opportunity to hurt Peter again. So Peter wants to know if there is a limit to forgiveness. Is there a point beyond which we do not need to forgive? Can we protect ourselves by refusing forgiveness?

Jesus says no. Jesus will not tell Peter it is all right not to forgive, and this should not surprise us. Jesus always challenges us by asking us to practice unreasonable love. He never tells us it is okay to love the people who are good to us but forget about those who hurt us. Quite the contrary, Jesus consistently calls us to practice a love that seems to ask too much of us; in fact, he's so unreasonable about love that he tells us we must even love our enemies. Sometimes forgiveness can seem the most unreasonable love of all, and we can list numerous convincing reasons why we ought not to forgive, but Jesus teaches that unless we are willing to risk the unreasonable, and sometimes even scandalous, love of forgiveness, death will get the best of us.

We seldom think of friends when we hear Jesus' admonition to love those who hurt us, but friendships can help us learn what it means to love those we find it hardest to love, even our worst enemies. First of all, aren't there times when even our best friends can seem more like enemies than friends? In the history of every friendship there are moments when the relationship is characterized by animosity more than benevolence, bitterness more than peace. Friends can hurt one another deeply. They can fail grievously all the proper expectations of friendship and drift into an alienation that seems unbreakable. When this happens, we not only wonder about the future of the friendship but also about how to describe the person we once took to be our friend. Is she now more enemy than friend? Whatever description abides depends on whether both of us are willing to work through the misunderstandings, hurts, and divisions and, through the hard work of forgiveness, rediscover the love that defined the friendship in the first place. In this sense, friendships teach us to love our "enemies" precisely so they may once again be our friends.

There is a second way friendships can embolden us to love those who do not seem to love us at all. Knowing that there are people, such as our friends, who truly care for us can give us the courage and confidence we need to risk loving those whose animosity for us we cannot deny. Knowing that our life is centered in friendships of genuine love and affection can give us the courage we need to reach out to those who may have done us great harm. In this respect, the love of friendship helps us not to hate our enemies but to pity them and, perhaps, to see them as more than the persons who have hurt us.

Still, we have to be careful about how we understand Jesus' call to nurture a forgiven and forgiving heart. In saying we should put no limits on our willingness to forgive, Jesus does not mean we should stay in situations that are unhealthy and harmful. Forgiveness ought always to be a path to new life, not annihilation. In counseling Peter always to be ready to forgive, Jesus does not intend for Peter to do nothing about relationships or situations that might be destructive. He does not want Peter to refuse forgiveness because he knows that if he says no to forgiveness he will die inside. But Jesus, who always calls us to choose life, in no way intends for any of us to stay in situations that bring death. Jesus tells us to love our enemies, not necessarily to live with them, and certainly never to allow them to destroy us.

This is why it is important to remember that there is an enormous difference between loving an enemy and loving our friends. Jesus summons us to love all our neighbors, but not in the same way. He tells us to love those who wish us harm, but never expects us to have the same loyalty, affection, and devotion for our seasoned enemies that we do for our lifelong friends. We love our friends with an intensity, depth, and joyfulness we obviously do not have with an enemy, because friendships originate in love and are meant to be a life together in love. We are challenged to love our enemies, but we would dishonor our friends if we showed to those who hate us the same affection and concern we owe our friends. Similarly, we may have to forgive an enemy, but much more is lost if we are unwilling to forgive a friend. The bond of love between friends, the history they have shared together, and the happiness they have brought one another indicate not only why forgiveness among friends is so crucial but also why Jesus never expects the love we risk on enemies to be equal to the love we shower on our friends.

Probing the Heart of God: The Parable of the Prodigal Son

Forgiveness may sometimes seem a preposterously unreasonable love to practice, but the Gospels make it clear that such unreasonable love does not begin with us but with God. No one loves more unreasonably than God does. No one loves with more reckless abandon than God does. We may be extravagant lovers, but we are no match for a God who refuses to allow millennia of waywardness to dampen his love. There is no more flagrant example of "love gone mad" than a God who is eternally ready to forgive when forgiveness makes no sense. When Christians forgive, it is only our feeble attempt to imitate the divine madness of a God who finds it much more life-giving to forgive than condemn. If God finds no joy in fostering bitterness or in harboring resentments, why should we?

This is the message behind the parable of the prodigal son, the infamous sinner-come-back-to-life of Luke's Gospel. What becomes clear in the story is that Jesus sees forgiveness not as weakness or defeat but as the incomparable, truly godlike power that frees us to deal with our lives in hope. Forgiveness means that the mistakes and misgivings of our lives do not have to be final and need not rule us. The parable of the prodigal son illustrates that forgiveness is not resignation but a *path to new life.* In fact, forgiveness is the most creative and innovative act of all, because it frees us to carry on in hope not by denying our past or even necessarily forgetting it but by reinterpreting it redemptively. Thus, forgiveness is not about forgetting, but about a new and more promising way of remembering.

Just like friendship, which is an ongoing way of life that involves growth in learning how to forgive, the story of the prodigal son illustrates that forgiveness is often not so much a single act but an ongoing process whose goal is reconciliation. The parable reveals five stages to the process of forgiveness. First, forgiveness begins with recognition of the alienation and brokenness wrought by sin. We see this vividly with the prodigal son. He left home, lived foolishly and ungratefully, wasted his fortune, his talents, and his gifts, and bottomed out in starvation and despair. The parable emphasizes his alienation by noting that the son is literally homeless, exiled in a "distant land," so removed from the normal ties of family and affection that while he starves "no one made a move to give him anything" (Luke 15:16). The son's sin placed him in absolute exile, so completely cut off from the life he once knew, as well as from all human companionship, that his only fellowship is with the pigs.

For forgiveness to work, it has to grapple with the alienation and brokenness that is the harvest of sin. This demands honesty. Luke says that eventually the prodigal son "came to his senses" (15:17) and began the journey home, but he was able to take that first step towards redemption only because he was also able to acknowledge his sin. He could have chosen to remain in exile, allowing a narrative of failure and foolishness to define the rest of his life. Wallowing with the pigs on a stranger's farm, he could have buried himself in self-pity and blame, proud in the conviction that resurrection would never be his. The parable would have a very different ending if the son had chosen self-pity over truthfulness, alienation over reconciliation; but if he had, the story would have ended in death, not fresh new life. What makes the prodigal son notable is not his chronicle of failure and defeat (who of us hasn't penned at least one chapter in that story?) but what he chose to do with it. The most important decision he made was not to let his foolish choices mark him forever and thereby skew the final chapters of his life. Instead, he chose to reconnect himself with life by seeking forgiveness and reconciliation from a father who had never stopped loving him.

The prodigal son was able to take that first step back to life when he could *reimagine* both himself and his life differently. This is the second stage in the process of forgiveness. His journey home begins when he reenvisions his life and himself, focusing not on his wickedness and loss but on what he was called to be from the beginning and now can be again. Unless we recover a clear sense of the self we have lost through sin and can, thanks to grace, embrace it again, we are too easily defeated by guilt and disgrace. Unless we can picture what we were and would like to be again, we surrender to the temptation that we can never be more than our failures. That is where sin wants to leave us, trapped in the ever deepening conviction that goodness, grace, and holiness—all the things that connect us to God and to life—can never be ours again.

Thus, forgiveness requires an act of the imagination. It requires that we envision something so much better and more promising for ourselves than the wrong we have done or the hurt we may have suffered. Forgiveness begins when we recover for ourselves a vision of the life, joy, goodness, and freedom God has never stopped wanting for us and is determined to give us. People who live a forgiven and forgiving life may be keenly aware of their own fallenness, but they keep their eyes fixed on a vision of hope they know to be both truer and more powerful.

It is when the prodigal son is able to imagine that the life he lost can be restored that he finds the energy he needs to break the chains of his captivity and begin his journey home. Realizing that even the "'hired hands at my father's place have more than enough to eat, while here I am starving!'" he awakes from his slumbers, leaves the pigs behind, and begins the convalescence that will reconnect him to life (15:17). Are we willing to entertain for ourselves the same vision of healing and life God wants for us? Are we willing to invest our hearts in a vision of brokenness overcome and communion restored? These are the questions each of us must answer in order to know the possibilities of forgiveness and reconciliation in our lives. So much of the healing that is possible for us depends on what we allow ourselves to imagine. We can choose to hold tight to images of ourselves as lost and defeated, wounded and broken for life, or we can choose to imagine ourselves healed, restored, and forgiven.

"Coming to his senses," the prodigal son chooses the image of himself forgiven and restored and lets that image carry him home. But before reaching home, his father, seeing his lost son approaching, is so overcome with joy that he rushes out to greet him. Throwing his arms around his son, he showers him with kisses, holds him tight with love, and joyfully welcomes him home. Before the once-lost son has even crossed the threshold, he is blessed with new life.

If we study this scene, what is striking about the father's response is that when the son returns home after wasting his inheritance and betraying his father's love, the father does not scold him for his sins; he does not berate him for his foolishness or remind him of what a failure he has been. No, the father's reaction is startlingly different. The very one who has most reason to be angry and to feel hurt and betrayed seems more overjoyed at the news of his son's homecoming than the son himself. And when he sees his son after all those years of separation, he does not utter one word about the son's failures. There is no mention of his sin, no probing of his mistakes. The father doesn't make the son beg, he doesn't ask him to go down on his knees and plead for forgiveness; in no way does he make his son feel small or embarrassed.

This is one of the most beautiful scenes in the Gospels, and perhaps it is one that has been reenacted in our own narratives of friendship. Like the father of the prodigal son, friends often display the graciousness of God's forgiveness by being eager, even overjoyed, to forgive. Some of the most poignant moments in any friendship come when the power of love overwhelms all feelings of bitterness and hurt. This parable speaks to all of us because, like the wayward son, we too have been humbled by the goodness of friends who utter no words about our missteps but speak only words of grace. It is at such moments that we realize anew not only the gift God has offered us in the friend but also how God's love so wondrously works through them.

Luke tells this story to show that the father does not care nearly as much about his son's failures as he does about forgiving him and welcoming him home. He is not interested in the wrong his son has done; he is only interested in his homecoming. He wants to bring his son who was "dead . . . back to life" (15:32). This is how the unreasonable love of forgiveness works. If we were writing the parable, it would seem reasonable for the father to say, "I will forgive you, but before you can cross the threshold and come home, I must tell you how badly you have strayed." It would seem reasonable, even just, for the father first to punish his son, and only then forgive him. But that's not how God's forgiveness works. God's forgiveness is patterned on the unreasonable love that does not count the cost, only the joy.

This brings us to the third stage in the process of forgiveness, namely the pivotal recognition that forgiveness is not our own achievement but is always absolutely a gift. The prodigal son knows he depends on his father's mercy. There is nothing he can do to merit forgiveness, nothing he can do to demand it. The prodigal son cannot unburden himself, nor can he free himself. His healing and unburdening will be the work of his father's mercy, not the result of his own determination. He cannot earn the gift of forgiveness, but he can be grateful for it. He cannot demand such mercy, but he can receive it, embrace it, and live in its freeing power. A key theme in the parable, and one we easily overlook, is that forgiveness begins with a gift. The question for the prodigal son, as well as for us, is what we are going to do with the gift.

Of course, the father in the story represents God, and the role of the father is to assure us that all forgiveness begins in the gift of God's mercy and gracious love. The word *for-give-ness* means exactly what it says: it is G*od's gift for us*, God's gift to heal us and set us free. Forgiveness is a *gift to live, a gift to enter into*. The father's offer of forgiveness does not mark the end of the prodigal son's journey, but its beginning; or perhaps better, forgiveness marks the end of his journey in sin and the beginning of his journey in new life.

It is no different with us. Forgiveness is God's gift for us, but it is a gift we are to enter into, a gift we are *to live from each* day of our lives. We are forgiven in order to live a forgiven and forgiving life. We are reconciled to God and others in order to live a reconciled and reconciling way of life. The parable makes this clear. The prodigal son is *first forgiven* and then begins his new life. The same is true for us. We do not first change our lives and then receive forgiveness; rather, it is the very fact of our having been offered forgiveness that enables us to live in new and better ways.

The parable of the prodigal son presents an immensely reassuring picture of God. Perhaps one reason this Gospel story strikes deep in our hearts, no matter how many times we have heard it, is because we absolutely depend on having a God who is like the father of the prodigal son, a God who is unconditionally forgiving, a God who will never say our failures are greater than his mercy.

Jesus tells the story to let us know that, as the father does, so God will always do. Like the father of the prodigal son, God stands watching for us to return. And like the father in this story, God loves us despite our shortcomings and accepts us with open arms. This is God's forgiveness: loving us despite our shortcomings, never letting those shortcomings be the last word about us, and accepting us with open arms. The parable tells us God will never not forgive, God will never close his heart to us.

Still, all this emphasis on the extravagant mercy of God may be reassuring, but it is also slightly troubling. It makes forgiveness seem too easy, perhaps too automatic and painless. It's great that the prodigal son is welcomed home, but it is almost as if he is rewarded for his transgressions. His father, giddy with the news of his son's return, showers him with kisses, clothes him with the finest robe, offers him new jewelry, sacrifices the fatted calf in his honor, and then tops off this spectacle of lavish mercy with a party. No wonder the ever faithful older brother is miffed. He's been the dutiful good son over the years, but when his dissolute brother has nowhere to turn and only then decides to come home, his father receives him as a hero. His brother's reconciliation seems too quick, too instantaneous; it is as if his monumental failures don't matter at all.

Is the parable nothing more than a seductive, but ultimately ill-advised, story of cheap grace? Is the son's extravagant homecoming the kind of quick consolation that tempts us to gloss over our failures so we might commit them again? A quick reading of the parable can suggest this, but closer scrutiny reveals that yes, forgiveness is an absolutely unmerited gift, but it also ought to be a *transformative gift*. Forgiveness is a grace, but a grace that ought to result in substantive changes in our lives— it is a grace that carries expectations. Forgiveness is not permission for the prodigal son to return to his past, but the freedom he needs to live a life of grace so that he does not have to repeat his past.

This brings us to the fourth stage of forgiveness, namely that the gift of forgiveness summons us to live a forgiven and forgiving life, a life of ongoing transformation and renewal markedly different from the life we embraced before. Look at the behavior of the father. Yes, he is overjoyed that his son "who was dead has come back to life," but it is also clear he expects his son to leave his dissolute habits behind. The father is quick to forgive because he knows real forgiveness marks a new beginning, not a careless return to the past. The father's expectation that his son will break with his past and take up a new kind of life is symbolized in the ritual where he vests his repentant son in new clothing and seals his homecoming by placing a ring on his finger. This is a sign that the son is welcomed home, but he is also expected to change. The vesting of the prodigal son in the new garment indicates not only a fresh start but also a break from a destructive and unpromising past. The ring signals a covenant in which the father's gift of forgiveness is to be met by the son's commitment to learning a new way of life.

It will not be easy. As L. Gregory Jones details in *Embodying Forgiveness*, living a forgiven and forgiving life is like an apprentice learning a craft.[4] It takes time, patience, study, and effort, plus the acquisition of new skills. In the Christian life, learning the craft of forgiveness means learning new attitudes, values, dispositions, virtues, and skills. It also means *unlearning* the very attitudes, values, dispositions, habits, and practices that led us into exile in the first place.

The prodigal son returns home and is welcomed with a feast, but then the hard work begins. If he honestly embraces the forgiveness that has been offered to him, he has to come to grips with his past self-centeredness, his embarrassing thoughtlessness, his blind ingratitude, and all his wastefulness and foolishness. He has to take account not only of the injustice he committed against his father but also of the understandable hurt and resentment suffered by the brother he left behind. He has to learn to live with a *contrite heart* and a *grateful spirit*, which suggests forgiveness is not a liberation that allows us to erase our past but a gift that enables us to redeem it.

It would be interesting to see how the story of the prodigal son continued. All the parable shows us is the first day of his new life. What we do not see is how the forgiven son settled into his new life once the celebration had ended. Was he able to *live into the forgiveness* that was his? Was he faithful to the gift? Did he make peace with his resentful brother? Could he see that living a forgiven and forgiving life is something like an ongoing convalescence, the slow rehabilitation of a life weakened by sin, depression, anger, or injury and strengthened by mercy, gratitude, graciousness, and love?

Suddenly the parable is not so heartwarming. It appeals to us when we focus on the exquisite mercy of the father, but it's a bit unsettling when we realize the robe and the ring symbolize the son's investiture into a way of life so radically different that it will be like learning to walk anew. If the prodigal son truly is to overcome his past and rise to new life, he must lean into a mercy that will not only transform him but will indeed give him a new identity, one so promising and challenging that he will hardly be able to recognize the self he used to be.

This is a great message, but one not easy to swallow because it tells us that real forgiveness is not a quick fix. It is the exquisite gift of God's remarkable mercy, but it is a gift that expects something from us. This is hard to accept because we have come to expect the same convenience from Christianity that we do from everyday life. We want fast absolution and quick reconciliation just as we want fast food. We want painless ways of dealing with the hurts, misdeeds, and disappointments of life just as we want painless ways of losing weight, fixing relationships, or making money.

Forgiveness may be quick, easy, and painless when we are dealing with the ordinary bumps and bruises of life (a thoughtless remark, a cutting comment, a missed appointment), but where the brokenness is deep and ravaging (a vow betrayed, a terrible injustice suffered, a loved one violently killed), forgiveness will only take root when we avail ourselves of the radically restorative life engendered by grace. It will only be sustained by difficult but ultimately healing virtues like gratitude, compassion, mercy, benevolence, and love.

We are no different from the prodigal son. Eventually our lives are wrecked on the shoals of some transgression either inflicted or endured, and we are faced with the question, How does life go on? Perhaps more concretely, How do friendships, left tattered by thoughtlessness and carelessness, go on? They go on when we allow ourselves to be apprenticed in the craft of forgiveness. The prodigal son was ready to take up that craft when he recognized his need for forgiveness and, with contrite heart, made his confession: "Father, I have sinned against God and against you; I no longer deserve to be called your son" (15:21). Similarly, we begin to live a forgiven and forgiving life when we are truthful about confessions that must be given or received (whether to friends, spouses, family members, colleagues, strangers, or even enemies), when we strive to live with a repentant spirit and a merciful heart, and, perhaps most important, when we commit ourselves to unlearning habits of domination, diminishment, self-deception, resentment, and bitterness and replace them with the liberating practices of justice, mercy, truthfulness, gratitude, peacefulness, and joy.

But we cannot do this alone. The fifth element to the process of forgiveness is that forgiveness requires the guidance, help, and assistance of others, especially those friends we know are truly concerned for our good. In order to live a forgiven and forgiving way of life, we need other people committed to helping us learn that life, who are there when we need help in dealing with the challenges and setbacks in living it. This is why there is such a close connection between friendship and a life of forgiveness. To live a forgiven and forgiving life, we need heartfelt friends, households of faith, and communities of encouragement, support, and truthfulness who help us navigate both the joys and the rigors of forgiveness. Other people—friends, communities, family members, and even strangers—are essential ingredients in living a forgiven and forgiving life because just as we cannot free ourselves from the hurts and misgivings of our pasts, neither can we alone sustain the ongoing healing and rehabilitation living into forgiveness entails. Without the help of friends, living a forgiven and forgiving life can seem too much for us.

Offering forgiveness is one thing, but keeping it alive is something else. Despite what we are often told, sometimes it is impossible to forgive and *forget*. How could parents forget that a drunk driver killed their child? How could a woman forget the violent assault of rape? How can a spouse forget the adultery of a partner? Forgiveness may be possible in each of these instances, but forgetting likely is not, and may even be unadvisable. Forgiveness is an ongoing process, and one of the things that can squelch the grace of forgiveness is the memory of hurts we have suffered or losses we have endured. No matter how resolved we might be to leave past hurts behind, we can be haunted by their memory and sometimes stunned at how fresh those memories can be. We may also feel we have left all bitterness and anger behind—guilt too—and be surprised at how quickly and unexpectedly they can erupt anew.

At these moments we have to decide to keep forgiveness alive, and yet realize we cannot do so by ourselves. But perhaps we can do this with the help of our friends. Especially when the hurts we have suffered or inflicted are extreme, forgiveness can never be once-for-all. It must be revisited, renewed, and reaffirmed as memories of the transgression surface and our souls feel bruised all over again. No one can sustain the grace of forgiveness without the guidance, patience, and support of friends. We need friends who will help us continue on in a life of forgiveness and who will protect us from returning to the tombs of past pains and old bitterness.

A powerful example of this is told in Sr. Helen Prejean's *Dead Man Walking*. At the end of the book Prejean relates a conversation she had with Lloyd LeBlanc, whose son David had been brutally murdered by one of the men Prejean befriended. LeBlanc tells her that when his son's killer, moments before his execution, asked for his forgiveness, he was ready to offer it because he already had forgiven him. On the night David was murdered, Lloyd went with the sheriff's deputies to the cane field where his dead son lay. Kneeling down by his son's body, Lloyd "prayed the Our Father. And when he came to the words: 'Forgive us our trespasses as we forgive those who trespass against us,' he had not halted or equivocated, and he said, 'Whoever did this, I forgive them.'"[5]

To even think about forgiveness at the moment he saw his murdered son's body is extraordinary, but Lloyd LeBlanc admitted that as difficult as it may have been to voice forgiveness that night, keeping the forgiveness alive was even harder. Forgiving in a single moment may be easier than continuing to forgive everyday, because when we offer forgiveness we do not always understand the cost it brings. We feel the cost of forgiveness when we are revisited by grief, when wounds we thought were healed open again, and when the losses we think we left behind kick us straight in our hearts. LeBlanc knew the price of forgiveness, "especially as he remembers David's birthday year by year and loses him all over again: David at twenty, David at twenty-five, David getting married, David standing at the back door with his little ones clustered around his knees, grown-up David, a man like himself, whom he will never know."[6] Hearing this, Prejean concludes: "Forgiveness is never going to be easy. Each day it must be prayed for and struggled for and won."[7] That is true, but as Lloyd LeBlanc's friendship with Sr. Helen Prejean showed, it is "prayed for and struggled for and won" not all by ourselves but together with the love, prayers, and support of our friends.

Conversely, other people can thwart the process of forgiveness for us if they refuse to offer us the mercy we need to live again. This brings us to the mystery character in the parable of the prodigal son—the miffed older brother. He has a right to feel angry and resentful—who of us wouldn't be?—but he has no right to stay that way. His younger brother cannot live the forgiveness he has been given without a changed heart in the brother he has hurt. He needs his brother to be able to move beyond his justified hurt and anger in order for both of them to live a truly reconciled life. This may not happen right away, but it has to happen eventually if alienation is not to abide between them and something much better and more important, namely the love they have to offer one another, is not to be lost. Thus, just as the prodigal son has a responsibility toward the brother he has hurt, so too does the injured older brother have a responsibility toward him.

The older brother cannot continue to hold the younger brother's past against him. He cannot, by refusing to forgive, condemn his brother to the mistakes of his past and say he can be nothing more than a brother who made a mess of his life, as if this could be the only truth about him. His responsibility is to see his brother in a much more hopeful and promising way, and he can do this only if he sees him not through eyes of bitterness and resentment but through eyes of mercy and compassion. Ironically, in order for the two brothers to live together in peace, the older brother must do what his younger brother has already done: he must see him differently, he must envision him not as a failure but as a blessed son of God with a potential for goodness, growth, and even holiness.

So much of forgiveness depends on the work of a gracious imagination. That is what is demanded of the older brother in the parable of the prodigal son, but it is frequently asked of all of us as we struggle to live a reconciled and reconciling life, especially with those who have hurt us. Can we reenvision those who have harmed us so that we see them as more than people who do harm? Can we change our perception of them, refocusing not on their failures and shortcomings but on the goodness, kindness, and love that also likely lives in them? So often when someone does us wrong (including our friends), our perception of that person becomes entirely negative. Instead of seeing the whole person, we zoom in on the harm she has done us and conclude this is the only way to see her. But to see her through the squinty vision of bitterness and resentment hardly does her justice. The grace of forgiveness, as well as the possibility of living a reconciled and reconciling way of life, demands that we "take another look." When we do, we discover anew that the people who hurt us are almost always people who also bless and do good. As Judy Logue writes, "Seeing a bigger picture makes room for a bigger story."[8]

Forgiveness and reconciliation occur when we are able to get new insight into those who have hurt us, and sometimes this fresh vision comes only through the hard work of prayer, an integral element to the life of friendship. Prayer is important for cultivating the gracious imagination necessary for forgiveness because through prayer we remember, for example, that we too have often stood in need of forgiveness from our friends and relied on them to offer it. Our friends may have hurt us, but we too have sometimes harmed and hurt our friends. We too have sometimes failed our friends, and when we did we were able to stumble forward only because they reached out to us with forgiveness. Nothing purifies our vision of others more than an honest reckoning of our own failures and renewed gratitude for the mercy we have received.

Moreover, prayer is indispensable for forgiveness because it reminds us, first, that all forgiveness, even our most feeble efforts, is rooted in the forgiveness of God. None of us forgives out of his own resources of mercy; rather, our forgiveness always shares in and flows from the forgiveness and mercy of God. When we forgive, God's forgiveness works through us to bless and heal another; we are at that moment instruments of God's healing Spirit. But prayer also teaches us that God has to be a partner to our forgiveness because otherwise we are not likely to find the strength, courage, and generosity we need to forgive. There are some things, like the murder of Lloyd LeBlanc's son, that seem instinctively unforgivable. When we hear of such atrocities, we often wonder how we would respond. Who of us could do what Lloyd LeBlanc did? Is forgiveness always possible?

The answer to that is, by ourselves—no; but with the help of God—yes. Left to ourselves, we do not have the resources to forgive, especially to forgive atrocities that seem utterly unforgivable. But Christians believe we are never left to ourselves because our forgiveness is rooted neither in our own goodness nor our own power but in the absolute goodness and powerful mercy of

God. Christians do not forgive because we are any better, nobler, or more merciful than others. We forgive because we live from the forgiveness of an absolutely forgiving God, and because God's mercy constantly supplies what is lacking in our own. It is our confidence in God's unending mercy that enables us to reach out to others and forgive.

When we forgive, we enact the parable of the prodigal son. Like the father of the prodigal son, we remove burdens and barriers from one another's lives. Like the father of the prodigal son, we free one another to take up life again. This is what makes forgiveness so powerful and so indispensable to the life of friendship. To forgive others is to grant them the power to take up life again. It is to free them from the imprisonment of shame and guilt so they can reconnect to life in hope. All of us must be able to do this. We need, always open before us, the possibility of picking up the pieces and starting over. Isn't this what Christianity is all about? Isn't it the religion of second chances and new beginnings? And shouldn't Christians, as people who know we live from mercy, extend that same gracious mercy to others?

These are truths to wrap our hearts around, and they express something of the wisdom that should accrue to Christians through worship. There is no more fitting context for learning the rubrics of a forgiven and forgiving life, because in worship we continually reenact and remember the paradigmatic expression of God's forgiveness in the crucifixion and death of his son. Entering into this story as completely as possible should make us a people who know well the absolute importance of forgiveness and reconciliation in a world often riven by bloodshed, divisions, and numbing cycles of violence. More than anything, it should make us a people who strive to embody forgiveness and mercy in our everyday lives and who do not hesitate to witness that forgiveness is the only reliable path to life we have.

Undoubtedly, forgiveness is often a preposterously unreasonable love, but our reason for hope is that God dared risk such preposterously unreasonable love with us. The community of the friends of God pledges never to forget that we live from extravagant mercy. This vow to remember well, like some eternal flame, fuels the gratitude that empowers us to live a forgiven and forgiving life, and, as the friends of God, to be a reconciling presence in the world. The church should be a sacrament of

God's forgiveness in our world. It should be the people who, standing at the foot of the cross, see in God, the wounded healer, a mercy that always triumphs over judgment. Keeping that memory alive in our hearts, the friends of God exemplify the words of Jesus, the master of forgiveness, who told his followers, "It is mercy I desire, not sacrifice" (Matt. 9:13).

Notes

Chapter 1

1. See Robert E. Webber and Rodney Clapp, *People of the Truth: A Christian Challenge to Contemporary Culture* (Harrisburg, Pa.: Morehouse, 1988), especially chapter 5, "Worship and Depth Politics," 68–83.

2. Walker Percy, *Love in the Ruins* (New York: Avon, 1978), 175.

3. Ibid.

4. Ibid.

5. Webber and Clapp, *People of the Truth*, 69.

6. I take this idea from Abraham J. Heschel's *Who Is Man?* (Stanford: Stanford University Press, 1965), 105–7.

7. Heschel, *Who Is Man?* 117.

8. Webber and Clapp, *People of the Truth*, 83.

9. Herbert McCabe, *What Ethics Is All About* (Washington, D.C.: Corpus, 1969), 126–73.

10. Ibid., 132.

11. Thomas Aquinas, *Summa Theologiae* (New York: McGraw-Hill, 1963–1969), III.79.1.

12. Ibid., III.73.3.

13. Ibid., III.73.5.

14. Enda McDonagh, *The Making of Disciples* (Wilmington, Del.: Michael Glazier, 1982), 39.

15. Ibid.

16. Cited from Stanley Hauerwas and William H. Willimon, *Resident Aliens* (Nashville: Abingdon, 1989), 83.

17. Webber and Clapp, *People of the Truth*, 56.

18. I take this term from James Alison's provocative and challenging book *The Joy of Being Wrong: Original Sin through Easter Eyes* (New York: Crossroad, 1998), 212–21.

19. Webber and Clapp, *People of the Truth,* 61.

20. For a remarkable and compelling analysis of the significance of the fruits of the Spirit for the Christian churches today, see Philip D. Kenneson's *Life on the Vine: Cultivating the Fruit of the Spirit in Christian Community* (Downers Grove, Ill.: InterVarsity Press, 1999).

21. Gerhard Lohfink, *Jesus and Community,* trans. John P. Galvin (Philadelphia: Fortress, 1982), 99–100.

22. I take this image of "exclusion and embrace" from Miroslav Volf's monumental work *Exclusion and Embrace: A Theological Exploration of Identity, Otherness and Reconciliation* (Nashville: Abingdon, 1996).

23. Dorothy Day, *The Long Loneliness* (New York: Harper & Row, 1952).

24. Tennessee Williams, *The Rose Tattoo* (New York: Signet, 1976), 178.

25. Ibid., 177.

26. National Conference of Catholic Bishops, *The Challenge of Peace: God's Promise and Our Response* (Washington, D.C.: United States Catholic Conference, 1983), #333.

27. Ibid., #331.

Chapter 2

1. William Nicholson, *Shadowlands* (New York: Plume, 1991), 82.

2. Aristotle, *Nichomachean Ethics,* trans. Martin Ostwald (Indianapolis: Bobbs-Merrill Educational Publishing, 1962), 1155a5.

3. Elizabeth Achtemeier, *The Committed Marriage* (Philadelphia: Westminster, 1976), 12.

4. Elaine Storkey, *The Search for Intimacy* (Grand Rapids: Eerdmans, 1995), 26.

5. Ibid., 10.

6. Ibid., 17.

7. Ibid., 18.

8. John Macmurray, *Persons in Relation* (Atlantic Highlands, N.J.: Humanities Press International, 1991), 105.

9. Ibid., 61.

10. Ibid., 61.

11. Emmanuel Mounier, *Personalism,* trans. Philip Mairet (Notre Dame, Ind.: University of Notre Dame Press, 1952), 20.

12. On this point, see Larry L. Rasmussen, *Moral Fragments and Moral Community: A Proposal for Church in Society* (Minneapolis: Fortress, 1993), esp. chapter 4.

13. Thomas Merton, "Love and Need: Is Love a Package or a Message?" in *Love and Living,* ed. Naomi Burton Stone and Patrick Hart (New York: Bantam, 1979), 26.

14. Ibid., 26.

15. Storkey, *The Search for Intimacy,* 21.

16. Ibid.

17. For a superb analysis of these ideas, see John F. Kavanaugh, *Still Following Christ in a Consumer Society* (Maryknoll, N.Y.: Orbis, 1992), esp. 3–61.

18. Storkey, *The Search for Intimacy,* 74–77.

19. H. Richard Niebuhr, *The Meaning of Revelation* (New York: Macmillan, 1941), esp. 44–54.
20. This idea was first suggested to me by Rodney Clapp. See his "The Celebration of Friendship," in *Reformed Journal,* August 1989, 11–13.
21. Kavanaugh, *Still Following Christ,* 65.
22. Ibid., 141.
23. On this point, see my *Friendship and the Moral Life,* 70–119.

Chapter 3

1. See Lawrence A. Blum, *Friendship, Altruism, and Morality* (London: Routledge & Kegan Paul, 1980), 192–95.
2. See Edward Collins Vacek, S.J., *Love, Human and Divine: The Heart of Christian Ethics* (Washington, D.C.: Georgetown University Press, 1994), 295.
3. For a fascinating account of this, see Nathaniel Branden, "Love and Psychological Visibility," in *Friendship: A Philosophical Reader,* ed. Neera Kapur Badhwar (Ithaca, N.Y.: Cornell University Press, 1993), 65–72.
4. C. S. Lewis makes this point in "Friendship—The Least Necessary Love," in *Friendship: A Philosophical Reader,* 41. "In each of my friends there is something that only some other friend can fully bring out," he writes. "By myself I am not large enough to call the whole person into activity; I want other lights than my own to show all his facets. . . . Hence true Friendship is the least jealous of loves."
5. Aristotle, *Nichomachean Ethics,* 1155a3–4.
6. Lewis, "Friendship," 46.
7. Marilyn Friedman, "Feminism and Modern Friendship," in *Friendship: A Philosophical Reader,* 298.

Chapter 4

1. Marie Aquinas McNamara, O.P., *Friendship in Saint Augustine* (Fribourg, Switzerland: University Press, 1958), 196–97.
2. Carolinne White, *Christian Friendship in the Fourth Century* (Cambridge: Cambridge University Press, 1992), 196.
3. Madeline L'Engle, *Two-Part Invention: The Story of a Marriage* (New York: Farrar, Straus & Giroux, 1988), 89.
4. Ibid., 100.
5. For a wonderful depiction of the "riddles of intimacy" in marriage, see Angela Huth's novel, *Invitation to the Married Life* (New York: Grove, 1991). For a deft analysis of what it takes to achieve intimacy in marriage, see Walter Wangerin Jr.'s *As For Me and My House: Crafting Your Marriage to Last* (Nashville: Thomas Nelson, 1987).
6. McNamara, *Friendship in Saint Augustine,* 197.
7. White, *Christian Friendship,* 201.
8. On this point, see Gilbert C. Meilaender, *Friendship: A Study in Theological Ethics* (Notre Dame, Ind.: University of Notre Dame Press, 1981), 17.
9. White, *Christian Friendship,* 202.
10. Ibid., 188.
11. Ibid., 194.

12. Peter Brown, *Augustine of Hippo* (Berkeley: University of California Press, 1969).

13. White, *Christians Friendship,* 215.

14. Ibid., 210.

15. Ibid., 209.

16. Ibid., 204.

17. Ibid., 205.

18. Ibid.

19. Ibid., 206.

20. Ibid.

Chapter 5

1. For the biographical details of Aelred's life, I have relied on Brian Patrick McGuire's *Aelred of Rievaulx: Brother and Lover* (New York: Crossroad, 1994).

2. Aelred of Rievaulx, *Spiritual Friendship,* trans. Mary Eugenia Laker, SSND. (Kalamazoo: Cistercian, 1977), 1:38. Subsequent references to *Spiritual Friendship* will be incorporated into the text.

Chapter 6

1. Cited in Vigen Guroian, *Ethics after Christendom: Toward an Ecclesial Christian Ethic* (Grand Rapids: Eerdmans, 1994), 11.

2. Vigen Guroian, *Incarnate Love: Essays in Orthodox Ethics* (Notre Dame, Ind.: University of Notre Dame Press, 1987), 53.

3. Austin Flannery, O.P., ed., *Lumen Gentium (Dogmatic Constitution on the Church), The Basic Sixteen Documents of Vatican Council II* (Northport, N.Y.: Costello, 1996), 5.

4. Ibid., 9.

5. Iris Murdoch, "The Sovereignty of Good over Other Concepts," in *The Sovereignty of Good* (London: Routledge & Kegan Paul, 1970), 77–104. Murdoch also demonstrated the importance but great difficulty of seeing truthfully in many of her novels, especially *The Sea, The Sea; The Good Apprentice; The Book and the Brotherhood;* and *The Message to the Planet.* For a theological analysis of the importance of vision in the Christian life, see Stanley Hauerwas, "The Significance of Vision: Toward an Aesthetic Ethic," in *Vision and Virtue: Essays in Christian Ethical Reflection* (Notre Dame, Ind.: Fides, 1974), 30–47; and Peter S. Hawkins, *The Language of Grace* (Boston: Cowley, 1983), 87–127.

6. Murdoch, *The Sovereignty of Good,* 37.

7. Murdoch, *The Sovereignty of Good,* 93.

8. Murdoch, *The Sovereignty of Good,* 67.

9. Ibid., 51.

10. For an excellent account of the meaning and importance of reverence for Christian ethics, see Dietrich von Hildebrand, *Fundamental Moral Attitudes* (New York: Longmans, Green and Co., 1950), 1–15.

11. Murdoch, *Metaphysics as a Guide to Morals* (New York: Penguin, 1992), 322.

12. Craig Dykstra, *Vision and Character: A Christian Educator's Alternative to Kohlberg* (New York: Paulist, 1981), 61.

13. Murdoch, *The Sovereignty of Good*, 67.
14. Murdoch, *Metaphysics as a Guide to Morals*, 339.
15. Dykstra, *Vision and Character*, 79.
16. Ibid., 80.
17. Rowan Williams makes this point in *Resurrection: Interpreting the Easter Gospel* (Harrisburg, Pa.: Morehouse, 1982), 114.
18. Jon Hassler, *North of Hope* (New York: Ballantine, 1990), 241–42.
19. Josef Pieper, *Faith, Hope, Love* (San Francisco: Ignatius, 1997), 100.
20. Ibid., 99.
21. Ibid., 91.
22. Ibid., 98.
23. Ibid., 91.
24. This is Pieper's definition of despair: "Despair is also an anticipation—a perverse anticipation of the nonfulfillment of hope: 'To despair is to descend into hell.'" Ibid., 113.
25. Ibid., 97.
26. Ibid., 116.
27. Henry Fairlie, *The Seven Deadly Sins Today* (Notre Dame, Ind.: University of Notre Dame Press, 1979), 113.
28. Pieper, *Faith, Hope, Love*, 118–19.
29. Ibid., 120.
30. Ibid., 122.
31. Thomas Aquinas, *Summa Theologiae* (New York: McGraw-Hill, 1966), II-II.17.1.
32. Ibid., II-II.17.8.
33. I am grateful to Sarabeth Gale, a student of St. Norbert College, for trying to verify the origins of this story.

Chapter 7

1. Bruce C. Birch, *What Does the Lord Require? The Old Testament Call to Social Witness* (Philadelphia: Westminster, 1985), 21.
2. Ibid., 38.
3. John R. Donahue, S.J., "Biblical Perspectives on Justice," in *The Faith That Does Justice: Examining the Christian Sources for Social Change*, ed. John C. Haughey (New York: Paulist, 1977), 76.
4. Birch, *What Does the Lord Require?* 27.
5. John C. Haughey, S.J., *The Faith That Does Justice*, 266.
6. Birch, *What Does the Lord Require?* 34.
7. Ibid., 50.
8. Ibid.
9. Ibid., 60.
10. Ibid., 55, 57.
11. Ibid., 57–58.
12. Ibid., 59.
13. Donahue, "Biblical Perspectives on Justice," 87.
14. On this point, see Haughey, "Jesus as the Justice of God," 282–88.
15. Ibid., 285.

16. *Justice in the World,* cited in *Catholic Social Thought: The Documentary Heritage,* ed. David J. O'Brien and Thomas A. Shannon (Maryknoll, N.Y.: Orbis, 1992), 289.

17. John A. Coleman, *An American Strategic Theology* (New York: Paulist, 1982), 24.

18. Thomas Aquinas, *Summa Theologiae,* II-II.58.1.

19. Pope John XXIII, "Christianity and Social Progress" (Mater et Magistra) #157 in *Catholic Social Thought: The Documentary Heritage.*

20. John Steinbeck, *The Grapes of Wrath* (New York: Penguin, 1967), 88.

21. David Hollenbach, *Justice, Peace, and Human Rights: American Catholic Social Ethics in a Pluralistic World* (New York: Crossroad, 1988), 193–94.

22. H. Kathleen Hughes, "Liturgy and Justice: An Intrinsic Relationship," in *Living No Longer for Ourselves: Liturgy and Justice in the Nineties,* ed. Kathleen Hughes, R.S.C.J. and Mark R. Francis, C.S.V. (Collegeville, Minn.: Liturgical Press, 1991), 51.

23. Hollenbach, *Justice, Peace, and Human Rights,* 200.

Chapter 8

1. Judy Logue, *Forgiving the People You Love to Hate* (Liguori, Mo.: Liguori, 1997), 20.

2. Ibid., 39.

3. Ibid., 43.

4. L. Gregory Jones, *Embodying Forgiveness: A Theological Analysis* (Grand Rapids: Eerdmans, 1995), esp. 207–39. Jones's book is the most comprehensive theological analysis of forgiveness to appear in recent years and poignantly demonstrates the centrality of forgiveness in the Christian life.

5. Helen Prejean, *Dead Man Walking* (New York: Vintage, 1994), 244.

6. Ibid., 245.

7. Ibid., 245.

8. Logue, *Forgiving the People You Love to Hate,* 65.